Living *with* Hope

*Navigating political divisions,
global pandemics, and
personal problems*

Dwight A. Moody PhD

LIVING WITH HOPE
NAVIGATING POLITICAL DIVISIONS, GLOBAL PANDEMICS, AND PERSONAL PROBLEMS

iUniverse books may be ordered through booksellers or by contacting:

iUniverse
1663 Liberty Drive
Bloomington, IN 47403
www.iuniverse.com
844-349-9409

All biblical quotations, unless otherwise noted, are from the New Living Translation, copyright @1996, 2004, 2015 by Tyndale House Foundation

ISBN: 978-1-6632-5455-9 (sc)
ISBN: 978-1-6632-5456-6 (e)

Library of Congress Control Number: 2023912928

Print information available on the last page.

iUniverse rev. date: 09/15/2023

Contents

Dedication

Marcy Mynatt, Reggie Headen, Michael Sebastian

with whom I have the delightful duty
of leading and serving the people of
Providence Baptist Church
Hendersonville, North Carolina

Introduction

These are consequential times. Christian people are engaged at every level of thought, word, and deed in this enterprise of living together as a nation. As we gather in sanctuaries and online to sing, pray, and hear the Word of God, we consider the momentous issues that confront us: life and death, wealth and poverty, war and peace, and the overarching challenge of the environment. We frame our thoughts and our actions in the context of God's mission in the world and our participation in that mission. We are called to be agents of justice, mercy, and humility, to seek first the rule of God, and to surrender ourselves to the exhilarating vocation of seeking the good of the human community from our platform within the Christian community. We are called to love God and to love our neighbor.

These grand callings come to us at Providence Baptist Church in Hendersonville, North Carolina. Yes, we are a little church—some thirty souls gathered for worship—and yes, we exercise little power or influence in the grand scheme of things. But we are also recipients of the promise articulated by the great apostle in his *Epistle to the Philippians:* that it was God who began a good work in us and through us, and it is God who will continue that good work until it is finished on the day that Jesus Christ appears. In this regard, we are very much like that first century congregation in Philippi—small, struggling, marginalized in the ebb and flow of imperial matters but convinced of the important work that God is doing in us, through us, and around us.

Like those first disciples, we struggle to build community, to embrace the Risen Lord as he comes to us, to practice generosity, hospitality, and humility, to listen to all the voices around us in our call to discern the times and to defend the Gospel. We make mistakes, get crossways with people, question the motives and means of others, and depend upon sometimes fragile connections to help us through the night, both literally and metaphorically. We treasure this letter from Pau, the apostle, to those who were first called Christians. We find in it the sustenance we need and the substance God designed for us and for them. For us and for them, it comes as the Word of God, deconstructing our lives, and, at the same time, connecting our spirits in ways that allow God to establish us as citizens of heaven.

I chose this letter for preaching and teaching material because it shares the concerns of our congregation as expressed in our slogan, *Sing for Joy, Live with Hope*. Joy and hope dominate this sweet letter, from the most famous hymn text in the New Testament (2:5-11) to the confidence that courses through the 4 chapters of the letter: confidence that God is at work, that God will give us life and freedom, and that God will bring together in gospel work the various actors depicted and described in the letter.

When we began this study of Paul's *Epistle to the Philippians* in January of 2022, we knew about the pandemic, but we did not know what else was coming: the war in Ukraine, the hearings of the House Select Committee on January 6, and the radical course launched by the Supreme Court to restructure much of our common life. The pandemic burdened our people and our congregational life: first, by emptying out the sanctuary, then by separating our people into those who came to the sanctuary for worship and those who did not. Then came the awful war, launched in February and brought home to us by the testimony of furloughing Ukrainian gospel workers Mina and Gennady Podgaiskys and by the persistent daily reports of all the news outlets.

The Congressional hearings about the January 6 Insurrection at the Capitol began in June and awakened the country to a deeper and more distressing understanding than what we had previously known. Even as I write this Introduction, the end is not in sight, even though the evidence of Presidential complicity mounts to overwhelming heights. Right in the middle of the hearings, the newly conservative Supreme Court unleashed its stunning reversals on prayer in public schools and privacy in the home and physicians' offices, while also embracing and expanding the practice of carrying weapons in public places. All of this brought increased attention to the rise and spread of Christian Nationalism.[1]

Even in these turbulent times, we are confident that God is at work in the surprising, even shocking events of our times. We are confident that God is at work in us as we read, listen, and proclaim the messages of this little letter. We are confident that God loves each and every one of us and also loves you. We are confident that God's purposes on this good earth (including in Hendersonville, North Carolina) are made plain to us in the reading and remembering of these ancient sentences. We are confident that God is able, in the very act of reading this letter and believing it, to make us wise to salvation—for us, for our families, for our nation, and for the whole world.

It is this salvation, this shalom, this kingdom life that we seek. Reading, praying and preaching through this letter brought it a bit closer. That is our testimony. We hope it is yours as well!

Finally, let me thank especially two people: Dr. Carol Pinkston, who carefully proofread this manuscript multiple times to ensure it was submitted with the highest degree of accuracy and clarity; and Ms. Holly Obermiller, who designed the book cover with all possible beauty and creativity. A long-lasting Thank You to both of these talented ladies.

---

[1] Christian Nationalism is a political ideology that has emerged in countries with long-standing Christian cultures (like the United States) and that seeks to gain political power to assert the rights and responsibilities of Christian people to shape the soul of a nation. Other countries have versions of Religious Nationalism, consistent with their religious histories and traditions. For sample advocates of Christian Nationalism, see Jason Rapert and his radio broadcast "Save the Nation" or the National Association of Christian Lawmakers.

One

The Good News of Christ

*Live as citizens of heaven, conducting yourselves
in a manner worthy of the good news of Christ.*
Philippians 1:27

Kentucky novelist Silas House has written a disturbing depiction of one possible future of our planet. *Lark Ascending* describes the journey of a young man (Lark), a dog (Seamus), and a woman (Helen) as they walk across Ireland, seeking safety from the violence and danger of a collapsed civilization. It is a dystopian vision of our future. Global warming has fueled fires around the world. What House calls "fundies" have taken over America—we might know these as Christian Nationalists. Dissent is suppressed by authoritarian governments, freedom is gone, and flight is the only option for those who do not abide by the religious and political values of the new overlords. Their journey is an arduous one, but it leads them to the once-Benedictine community that has survived the brutality and maintained the practices of hospitality and compassion.

Much in our common life today tends in the direction of this depressing story. All around us there is trouble. Into this rising tide of bad news, we gather each week to *sing for joy and live with hope.* We come to worship the living God, to remember Jesus, the Risen

1

Lord, and to open ourselves to the Spirit of life and love. In other words, we are gospel people—good news people—believing that the power God used to raise Jesus from the dead is accessible to us and to everyone.

Paul, the great apostle, speaks to this when, in the short letter written almost 2,000 years ago, he challenges us to be people "conducting ourselves in a manner worthy of the Good News." He calls us "to stand together with one spirit and one purpose." That is the kind of person I want to be, and that is the kind of believing community we want to be. That is why, today, *we sing for joy and live with hope.*

We declare our faith: God is present in and among us! God is powerful in and through us. God has a purpose for us and for the whole world.

I.

I want you to be a teller of good news, gossiping the Gospel, we might say.

I am grateful that often when I was a child, people told me the story of Jesus: my parents, my teachers, my church leaders. Everyone in the world needs to know the story of Jesus. God sent Jesus as teacher, healer, friend of saints and sinners, and savior of the world. Jesus died on a cross, was buried in a borrowed grave, and on the third day, God raised him from death to life. The story of his birth, his life and ministry, his teaching, his prayers, his arrest and death and resurrection is a story for everyone. I'm glad somebody told me. Are you glad somebody told you?

How can we be tellers of the good news?

Here is what we want to tell: *God raised Jesus from the dead. God affirms and vindicates the life and ministry of Jesus and his practice of unbounded love. God offers this same Spirit of unbounded love to you,*

*and me, and everyone. God promises a future of unbounded love—what
is sometimes called "beloved community"—to the whole human race.*

We believe this good news, and we seek to live in it. This
empowers us to *sing for joy and live with hope*, especially when our
world is beset with so much violence and pain, so much instability
and uncertainty, so much danger and disease.

This year, floods brought death and destruction to Eastern
Kentucky. As a Kentucky native and a long-term Kentucky resident,
my heart grieved. In Perry County, the rains turned into floods and
pushed the North Fork of the Kentucky River out of its banks. That
river snakes in and around Harlan, Kentucky, a region of poverty
and deprivation. This flood has brought more death, more loss, more
grief, more despair, and more need.

In times like these, the world needs people who sing for joy
and live with hope. It needs people with good news. It needs
citizens of heaven, who live as if the power that raised Jesus from
the dead is capable of overcoming division, renewing friendships,
empowering compassion, producing generosity, sustaining sacrifice,
and welcoming strangers.

II.

Let's begin with Jesus. Jesus taught the love of God. God loves
you. We are to love God and love one another. This love is an
awareness of the value of each person. It is an empathy for the
struggle of each and every person. It is a commitment to act in the
best interest of each person.

That is the meaning of the story Jesus told of the man beaten
by thieves and left to die. It is also a story of the stranger who
happened by and tended to his wounds. We call him the Good
Samaritan.[2] We all aspire to live and act that way: to be courageous
and compassionate in times of crisis and confusion. To tell this story

---

[2] The story is found in *Luke*, chapter 10.

3

is to share the good news. To embody this story is to *be* the good news.

Living in the presence of God is the key to abundant life and life eternal. We are made for God, and our hearts are restless until they rest in God. We are called to live in beloved community: to love God and love our neighbor. To be gospel people is to treat everyone as our neighbor: our white neighbor and our black neighbor, our Christian neighbor and our Muslim neighbor, our rich neighbor and our poor neighbor, our straight neighbor and our gay neighbor. Everyone in the world is our neighbor. We are to act and vote and pray, thinking about our neighbors down the street and our neighbors around the world.

People killed Jesus and discredited his life. Some skeptics asked: "How can the blessing of God be on a person who died as a criminal on a cross?"

To signal his approval of Jesus and his message of love, God raised Jesus from the dead. It was the public stamp of approval from God upon Jesus. God took his stamp, pressed it into a holy inkpad, and stamped on Jesus: **Approved**. God declares: "Pay attention to Jesus because I affirm who he is, what he did, and what he said."

This resurrection power of God flows from Jesus around the world and through history. The Bible tells one long story of where that power made a difference, bringing life out of death, freedom out of bondage, power out of weakness, grace out of judgment, righteousness out of wickedness, and hope out of despair.

We are gospel people. We are good news people. We are Jesus people. We declare Jesus is Lord, risen from the dead, alive and at work all around us. Thanks be to God!

III.

God is also present in our congregation, not just out there in the world somewhere, and not just back there on that first Easter.

God is present: calling us together, calling us *to sing with joy and live with hope,* calling us to love and understand one another, and calling us to pour out our lives for the good of our community and the flourishing of our world.

Yes, I know we are small. On any given Sunday, no more than a couple dozen people gather in our sanctuary. That makes us a small congregation by some standards. Yes, there are large megachurches scattered around the world. Most of the large urban centers have huge congregations: Seoul in Korea, London in Great Britain, Sao Paulo in Brazil, Houston in Texas, Nairobi in Kenya, Rome in Italy. But we—Providence—are more like the church in Philippi to whom Paul wrote this letter. We are a small church, a micro-church, some say today. But there are millions of congregations like us around the world, just as there have been millions of them down through the centuries.

We are the wave of the future. Many large churches are now small churches. One member of our church is a church architect. He said to me last year, "Most of our work these days is helping megachurches downsize and offload property." I recently came upon a video of the largest church in the United States: Joel Osteen's Lakeside Church in Houston. The camera from behind the preacher scanned the audience. You know what I saw? Empty seats! Five years ago, you would see no such thing in that large arena. Every church I know has downsized!

We *sing for joy and live with hope* in our small congregation. We have a great confidence that God has brought us here for a purpose. Even though we are a minority voice in the Christian community, we are tearing down barriers, welcoming people, and empowering everyone. We are the church of the future!

Sometimes we hear it said, "The first confession of faith among those early Christians was, Jesus is Lord." This may be true. But some scholars think otherwise.[3] They contend that the earliest of all

---

[3] See Stephen J. Peterson, *The Forgotten Creed: Christianity's Original Struggle against Bigotry, Slavery, and Sexism* (Oxford: Oxford University Press, 2018. I credit Diana Butler

confessions of faith was this: "There is no longer Jew and Gentile, slave or free, male and female. For you are all one in Christ Jesus" (*Galatians* 3:28).

Paul's insertion of this in *Galatians* addressed the first major crisis of the Christian movement: shall we let them in? Those first followers of Jesus were Jews, and they did not want others—Gentiles—to join their movement, unless they first became Jews. They must be like us, they said. *Acts of the Apostles* chapter 15 and *Galatians* chapter 2 describe and discuss this controversy. Shall we keep the circle small and exclude them? Or shall we make the circle large and include them?

The Christian community in the United States is now engaged in a great civil war on the same question. The United Methodist Church is splitting over the issue. A generation ago, it was the Episcopal Church splitting. Now, even the Pentecostal movement, one of the more conservative, is grappling with this question: are we all one in Christ?

Here at Providence, we have a great mission and a great message. It is our moment to *sing for joy and live with hope*! God has brought us here for this purpose and with this message. There is resurrection power among us, in us, around us, and through us. This resurrection power of God enables us to overcome prejudice, to undermine hatred and bigotry. This resurrection power equips us to love and understand one another and practice hospitality to all whom God sends our way.

We are not trying to take over the United States. We are not creating armed militias and training survival groups. We are not abandoning our Christian mission for a political uprising. Rather, we are gathering to pray and sing and give and serve. We are the hands and feet of Jesus. We are the resurrection of Jesus for our day and time. Thanks be to God.

Bass for recommending this book during a presentation at the Southern Lights 2022 conference at Epworth by the Sea on St. Simons Island, Georgia.

IV.

The resurrection power of God raised Jesus from the dead. The resurrection power of God is energizing our congregation to *sing for joy and live with hope.* But that same resurrection power also inspires us as individuals to see God more clearly, to love God more dearly, and to follow Jesus more nearly day by day. Those are lyrics from the rock musical, *Godspell,* that our associate pastor quotes with some frequency. It is a song based on a prayer of a 13th century English bishop named Saint Richard of Chichester. It can be our prayer today.

What we want is transformation. We want God to make us the people God wants us to be. We ask ourselves, what kind of person is that?

I know of no better answer to that question than the 8 **I-Sayings** of the Apostle Paul found in chapters 3-4 of *Philippians.*

Paul begins his list with "**I never get tired**" of doing gospel work, words we all can embrace. When he reviewed his religious resume, complete with his adherence to all the requirements of temple and synagogue, he said, "**I consider it trash.**" Instead, it is faith in the living God that lifts us to salvation and service.

"**I want to know Christ and experience the mighty power that raised him from the dead,**" Paul wrote, expressing for all of us a good gospel aspiration. "**I press on,**" he said as he reflected on his past, his present, and his future. God has called us, and we also press on to take hold of that high calling. He followed that with "**I love you ..., dear friends.**" I say to you as your pastor, I love you all, and I like most of you, also!

"**I praise the Lord**" is perhaps the easiest of all of Paul's **I-Sayings** for us to embrace. We love to praise the Lord because we *sing for joy and live with hope.* Then, we come to this I-saying, featured today by our vocalist: "**I can do everything through Christ who gives me strength.**" You will find it, first, in *Philippians* 4:13, but you will

7

find it more often buried deep in the hearts and minds of Christian people like us. It is a treasured statement of our faith.

Finally, we come to what I call the most counterculture of all of these attitudes. In our environment of consumption, accumulation, and storage bins, Paul says for all of us, "**I have all I need.**"

These 8 sayings, buried in these beautiful lines of this wonderful letter, are signposts on our journey to personal transformations. Repeat them. Pray them. Post them on the walls of your house and the doorposts of your home. Bury them deep in your soul, and let them seep out into what you say, how you react, and where you go. These 8 **I-Sayings** will help you *sing for joy and live with hope.*

By the resurrection power of God, they will make you a gospel person and will make us a good news congregation. In the power of the spirit of God, we will *sing for joy and live with hope.*

Two

The Work of God

*God will continue the work until it is finished
on the Day when Christ Jesus returns.*
Philippians 1:6

In the famous French novel, *Les Misérables*, several story lines are
intertwined to form one of the most captivating dramas in modern
Western culture. In the British adaptation for musical theater, the
fulcrum of action is the battle at the barricades. Marius casts his
lot with those young revolutionaries who have organized to push
back against the social and economic conditions of their day. The
French soldiers commissioned to maintain order and suppress such
uprisings meet them at the barricade. Underneath this larger cultural
and political drama is the love story of Marius and Cossette, and,
of course, the conversion story of Jean Valjean. Will Marius survive
the battle to take Cossette as his bride? Will Jean Valjean escape the
pursuit of Javert to live in peace?

I.

This novel features the tension between the public, the historical, and the cultural drama that shapes our world, on the one hand, and on the other hand, the personal, daily drama that shapes our lives. This same kind of tension also runs all the way through the biblical narrative. It oscillates from one to the other.

Think of Moses, alone on the backside of the wilderness, confronted with a bush that would not burn up and a voice that could not be ignored. The next act finds him face to face with the most powerful ruler in the world, the Pharaoh of Egypt. Moses is decrying the conditions in which his people live. He is demanding that things change.

Think of John, the baptizing prophet, who was also the cousin of Jesus, leading his religious movement on the outskirts of civilization. Hundreds of people left their homes and synagogues to go to his outdoor revival meetings, listening to his call for moral reform, and watching him immerse people in the waters of the Jordan River. But then, John turns his attention to the ruler of the realm, a man named Herod, ruling as king of the Jews. John called him out and called him down. But it was Herod who had the final say; he took John in, so to speak, and then took him out![4]

That same tension between the personal and the public is part of what it means to be a human, to be an American, even to be a citizen of the world. We grow up, find a job, marry, raise a family, and struggle to balance the social, the romantic, the financial, and the physical. Pressing upon us are the national issues: politics, investments, trends, movements, and demands, alongside opportunities to relieve suffering, reform society, address pandemics, and save the planet.

We encounter that same personal/public dynamic on almost every page of the Bible, in every day in the life of Jesus, and in

---

[4] The story of how John's preaching troubled Herod and how Herod eventually murdered John is told in the *Mark* 6:14-29.

understanding the life and message of Paul, the apostle. We open *Philippians* and read its wonderful words. Most of them seem to focus on the personal side of life and religion; but underneath it, around it, and through it are larger issues, empire issues, global issues.

Paul writes about Timothy and Epaphroditus, but he is writing from jail, incarcerated by some civil authority for disrupting the peace. He urges Euodia and Syntyche to settle their dispute, but he sends greetings from Caesar's household. He greets the believers with their leaders and assistants, but he is organizing cells of people who believe new things and practice new things, part of a movement that will eventually rule the world. He talks about what it means to be "in Christ"—a relationship with God through Christ that is transformational of character and behavior. Then he gears it all to a bigger-than-life event that he calls the Day of the Lord Jesus Christ: a global event, a historical event big enough to end the age and launch another.

This is the canvas upon which Paul paints what he sees as the work of God in the world. What indeed is God up to in your life, in your church, in the world? Paul says God has begun a good work, and God will complete this good work.

II.

It is not often that I resort to the Greek to make a point in a sermon. But here is one case where the Greek language is crucial. The English phrase *in you* obscures the Greek. Is that word *you* singular or plural? Is the great apostle speaking of what God is doing in you as a person, as an individual, as a believer who traces your Christian life from "the hour you first believed" (to quote the famous gospel song)?

Or is it plural? Is the meaning *among all of you*? That is, is God doing a good work in your congregation, your community of faith, among all the believers in Philippi or in Hendersonville, or in the United States, or even in the entire world?

You see immediately the difference it makes. To borrow from the poet, two roads diverge from this linguistic wood, and the one you take makes all the difference. Either you take the road to personal and privatized religion, or you take the road to public and global religion.

Our tradition has been quick to take the former, to read this text and others like it, focusing on the personal dimension of our Christian faith and practice. We read the gospel story and apply it to us. This is the power of the gospel song:

I was sinking deep in sin, far from the peaceful shore…
Love lifted me. Love lifted me.
When nothing else could help, love lifted me.

I have a collection of books that detail conversion stories: Thomas Merton and *The Seven Storey Mountain*, Chuck Colson and *Born Again*, and C. S. Lewis and *Surprised by Joy*. Think of the testimony of the late vampire novelist Anne Rice. A personal testimony is a powerful thing. The unnamed woman whom Jesus met at the well went back to her village and testified to others of her encounter with Jesus.

I have a testimony like these. It is not as dramatic, but it is every bit as personal and powerful and transformational.

I hope you have a story of your journey with Jesus. I hope you can testify today of something that happened this past year or even this past week that pulled you back from despair, pushed you toward a surprising future, or prompted you to get something in your life cleaned up or cleared out. I hope you can stand and say today,

Jesus walks with me and talks with me and tells me I am his own!

III.

The point is this: the Greek here in *Philippians* is not *in you*. It is *among us*. It is plural.

Paul was writing from jail in Rome, probably, to a small and struggling band of believers in Philippi. God was saying through Paul that God is at work: in their faith community, their little church; among them in their network of home gatherings; and through them as they gathered weekly to eat the fellowship meal, to read the letters of Paul as they were copied and distributed throughout the churches, to recount the stories of Jesus, and to care for people in the stress and strain of life. But most of all, he was writing to people who had quit saying "Caesar is Lord" and had begun saying "Jesus is Lord."

These were communities of people who had been baptized into an alternative way of being people, of being community, of being citizens—not of the empire but of heaven, not in obedience to the governor or the emperor but to the Crucified One, to the Risen Lord, to Jesus who is coming again to complete the work of transforming the world.

It is easy to domesticate this sweet little letter to the Philippians. It is easy to reduce it to a devotional tract about peace of mind, mending friendships, and giving cheerfully. All of those things *are* here. We will read them, one by one, and meditate on them and seek to practice them in obedience to the command of Jesus.

What we need is a wide-angle lens to puts things in perspective. The recent book *Factfullness*[5] does exactly this.

Factfulness is a word coined by the book's author, Hans Rosling, to signal his laser focus on gathering data. He was a Swedish physician who spent his life as a global health specialist. He died in 2017, just after launching a non-profit center called the Gapminder

---

[5] Hans Rosling, Ola Rosling, Anna Rosling Ronnlund, *Factfulness: Ten Reasons We're Wrong about the World—and Why Things Are Better Than You Think* (New York: Flatiron, 2018).

Foundation. The Foundation is committed to gathering the data about the social and economic conditions of the world.

The results may surprise, even shock you. Tracking the date from 1800 to 2020—220 years—we learn that legal slavery decreased dramatically, from 193 countries to 3! Only 4% of children die before their 5th birthday compared to 44% in 1880.

Since 1940, deaths from disaster have decreased from 971,000 per year to 72,000 per year. Deaths by plane crash have decreased from 2,160 per billion passengers to 1 per billion passengers. Since 1970, the percentage of people in the world who are undernourished has decreased from 28% to 11%. We are living in one of the most peaceful periods in modern history with only one battle death per 100,000 population per year.

The decline in trauma and tragedy is only half the story; the other half is triumph and success. The number of countries where women have won the right to vote has increased from one in 1893 to 193 in 2017. The percentage of earth's land surface protected as parks and reserves has increased from .03% in 1900 to 14.7% in 2016.

Since 1980, the percent of people with internet access has increased from 0% to 48%. The percent of one-year-old children who received at least one immunization has gone from 22% to 88%. Over the last 25 years, the share of people with some access to electricity has gone from 72% to 85%, and the share of people with water from a protected source has gone from 58% to 88%.

Even with all this encouraging news, we acknowledge that there are problems in the world and in the United States. Some today are warning of a decline in democratic societies and of a rise in totalitarian regimes. I do not discount this, and we must always be vigilant and engaged in the struggle for justice, for life, and for peace.

III.

This wide-angle perspective on global conditions pushes us to take a wide angle look at our faith, at the Christian community. First, it tells us that sometimes God is at work around and not through the Christian community, sometimes in spite of the Christian community, and sometimes in the face of resistance from the Christian community.

Sixty years ago, it was the Christian communities in the South that stood in the doorway and said to the Civil Rights marchers, "No way!" In our day, too many Christian communities have sat in their sanctuaries and said to the Public Health officials, "No way! We are not staying home! We are not wearing masks!"

Sometimes, God must go around us!

But God also is working among us, throughout the world to declare Jesus risen from the dead and to pledge our allegiance not only to the global community but also to our heavenly citizenship.

In 2022, the people of South Africa laid to rest the Nobel Prize-winning preacher who led the way against segregation and corruption. Desmond Tutu was a citizen of the world. He was buried in the cheapest pine box on the market. People sang the songs of Zion. God worked through him and through those who marched with him and prayed with him and sang with him. May God raise up more people like Desmond Tutu.

God is working among you, Providence Baptist Church. I know you have despaired. I know you have looked around sometimes and wanted to cry. The church used to be full of people: children and visitors and those seeking the Lord. Do not be dismayed.

In a minute, we are going to sing a great hymn. "God make you joyful everyone, let nothing you dismay!" What a wonderful song... for Providence. It picks up the twin themes of this delightful letter: consolation and joy. I have edited the title and first line to make this

15

clear to us, many centuries after it was written: "God Rest Ye Merry, Gentlemen" has become "God Make You Joyful, Everyone."[6]

God who began a good work among you 20 years ago[7] will complete that good work: in us and among us and around us and through us. God has brought us to this place and to this time. What God has in store for us, among us, through us, and around us is the wondrous mystery of life.

Let us celebrate, in the words of the great old prayer of Francis of Assisi.

Lord, make us an instrument of Your peace
Where there is hatred, let us give love.
Where there is injury, let us grant pardon.
Where there is doubt, let us practice faith.
Where there is despair, let us live with hope.
Where there is darkness, let us light the way.
Where there is sadness, let us sing for joy.

---

[6] The hymn with no known writer appears as early as the 16th century, the Wikipedia article explains. The original meaning of the opening line was "God grant you peace and happiness" as in "God rest (make) you merry (happy), gentlemen (people). I heard this history and interpretation at the Presbyterian Church on St. Simons Island during the 2021 Christmas holidays.

[7] Providence Baptist Church was founded in 2001, with Rev. Gail Coulter as pastor. The congregation celebrated its 20th anniversary in July of 2021, when I was serving as Sunday Preacher. Now retired, Rev. Coulter remains an active and honored member of the congregation.

Three

The Hour I Last Believed

You have been my partners in spreading the Good News about Christ from the time you first heard it until now.
Philippians 1:5

Some years ago, I led a preaching series for a congregation that featured testimonies by church members. We used as our theme, *The Hour I First Believed*. This is a line from the famous gospel hymn, *Amazing Grace*.

That hymn grew out of the conversion of its author, John Newton. He was a ship's captain in the infamous triangle: bringing Africans to America, taking raw materials to England, and delivering finished products to Africa. During one trip, his ship was caught in a terrible storm. Fearing it would sink, Newton prayed for deliverance and forgiveness. The storm subsided, but the spiritual stirring in his soul had just begun.

He counted March 10, 1748, as the day he first believed.

I.

Do you recall the hour you first believed?

Many of us cannot, because (as Paul once wrote to Timothy: "you have been taught the holy Scriptures from childhood, and they have given you the wisdom to receive salvation" (*Second Timothy* 3:16). Paul mentions that Timothy's mother and grandmother were both followers of Jesus Christ as Lord. Such is my story, and it may be yours.

But I do recall the revival meeting that stirred my heart. I remember talking to my father and kneeling beside a bed to pray. I remember the waters of baptism and what the pastor said before he dipped me under.[8] Do you remember the hour you first believed?

Paul remembered the hour the Philippians first came to faith in Jesus Christ. He wrote this: "You have been my partners in spreading the Good News about Christ from the time you first heard it until now" (1:4). He had in mind not only the change in their thinking and living but also the change in their giving. Not only did their minds and hearts get converted, so did their wallets.

One person said as he entered the baptismal pool, "Oh, I forgot to take my wallet out." He reached as if to pull it out and put it aside. But the pastor was wise and quickly said, "No, leave it in. It also needs to get converted!"

Paul is effusive in his praise of the Philippians. Throughout the letter, he mentions their generous support of his gospel work and travels. In chapter 2, he mentions Epaphroditus and writes, "He was your messenger to help me in my need" (2:25). At the end of the letter, he writes, "You Philippians were the only ones who gave me financial help when I first brought you the Good News and then traveled on from Macedonia. No other church did this. Even when I was in Thessalonica you sent help more than once" (4:15). Paul celebrated the way the Philippians had been converted, thoroughly

---

[8] My pastor, Rev. Clarence Walker (1890-1968) of the Ashland Avenue Baptist Church of Lexington, Kentucky, baptized me in March of 1960. I was just about to turn ten years old.

converted: their affections, their convictions, their habits, and their spirit of generosity.

Someone has said that the world population is divided into givers and takers. Either these ancient Philippian people were, by nature and disposition, givers, or their powerful and sustained encounter with Jesus, the Risen Lord, had taken their once stingy instincts and transformed them into habits of holiness and grace and generosity.

"God loves a person who gives cheerfully," Paul wrote to the church at Corinth in his second letter to them (9:7). But he could have written it to the church at Philippi and also the church at Hendersonville. Paul could have also written "God loves a cheerful and generous giver." And so do we, don't we?

From the hour they first believed, they were cheerful and generous givers.

II.

One of the strange things about this letter is what is not included. Nowhere in this letter does Paul mention the events at Philippi as described in the *Acts of the Apostles*. He does not even allude to them in any way.

Two of the most famous stories from that first century of Christian living happened in Philippi, according to chapter 16 of *Acts of the Apostles*.

Paul and Silas left Asia and entered Europe. They crossed the Aegean Sea and found their way to northern Greece, to Macedonia, to the town of Philippi. They went to the river and there found Lydia, leading a prayer meeting. Today, prayers are offered in temples, churches, mosques, and synagogues. These are led by religious professionals and funded by gifts to the institution.

But here by the river in Philippi, people were praying. Perhaps they were reading and testifying and asking questions and probing for answers. We have no details, but we know that the message of

Paul, of Jesus risen from the dead, resonated with Lydia. She offered first her attention, then her allegiance, then her home. She was the first convert in Europe.

But there is no mention of her in *Philippians.*

Later, Paul cast out an evil spirit from a woman. The commotion that followed landed him in jail. Silas was with him, and the story in *Acts of the Apostles* describes them singing hymns at midnight.

Isn't that a wonderful idea! Singing is a powerful form of Christian testimony, a splendid way to describe the wonder of God and the story of Jesus. That is one reason we have as part of our theme, *Sing for Joy.*

While they were singing, the earth quaked, and the earth shook. The event struck fear into everyone. The jailer hurried to Paul and Silas and asked, "Can you save us? How can we survive?"

The writer reports that Paul told them the good news of Jesus, the One sent from God, who went about doing good, who calls us to repentance, love, generosity, and the kingdom of God wherein we are all neighbors. That man and his family heard the testimony, believed the Good News, and asked to be baptized.

But there is no mention of this in *Philippians.*

It is reasonable to think both the praying woman named Lydia and the believing man who is not named were still members of the Christian community in Philippi, but neither is mentioned in this letter. There is no notice at all, no subtle hint, not even an allusion, except for this fact: those two episodes established a tradition of generosity and hospitality that carried on. Both the praying woman and the seeking man invited the apostle into their homes. These qualities reflect the spirit of Jesus, the teaching of Jesus, the presence of Jesus. These qualities—generosity and hospitality—make for a congregation of people filled with the Spirit and walking in the Way. Generosity and hospitality were in the DNA, we would say today, of what Paul describes as "the holy people in Philippi who belong to Christ Jesus" (1:1).

That is the kind of Christianity that is compelling. That is the kind of church that is attractive. That is the kind of human community that pulls people in and shapes them into those who love God and love their neighbor. That is the kind of congregation where people are eager to tell the story of the hour I first believed.

III.

But today, it is not *the hour I first believed* that makes the headlines but *the hour I last believed.* People are giving up on religion, church, Jesus, and God.

A few years ago, a Houston man published a book entitled *Goodbye Jesus.* His name is Tim Sledge. He was a seminary-educated minister and pastor of a Baptist church for 30 years. But then life got complicated, and church life got uncomfortable, and Christian life became unbearable. He quit church. He quit Jesus. He quit God. I interviewed him in The Meetinghouse. You can listen to our 48-minute podcast at themeetinghouse.net.[9] It is his testimony of *the hour I last believed.*

Tim Sledge is one of many. Scholars tell us that millions of people have given up on God. The percentage of unbelievers in the United States has gone from 19% of the population to 29% of the population in ten years. And for the first time in American history, fewer than half of the population are connected to a house of worship of any kind. During the pandemic, in sanctuary worship attendance declined by 30%.[10]

Yes, some people pulled away from church because of the pandemic. We were all encouraged to protect ourselves. "Stay home from anything and everything if you do not feel safe," we said to one

---

[9] TheMeetingHouse is a media platform I launched in 1998, while on the faculty of Georgetown College. It now includes a website, a weekly newsletter, and a video broadcast/podcast.

[10] See, for instances, the Pew Research Center report of October 17, 2019, and March 22, 2022, both at www.pewresearch.org.

another. Along with many churches, we launched a video broadcast to keep our people connected to church, to friends, to Scripture, to prayer, and to Jesus.

Yes, other people have pulled away from church because community life with people is messy. People are not easy to know and love. Some people, even some believing people, are toxic; they are self-centered and unhappy.

Some people in the Philippian church were like that. Each of the 4 chapters in this little letter addresses some element of the difficulty of staying in fellowship with people.

In chapter 1, Paul mentions jealous people. In chapter 2, he warns us of selfish people. In chapter 3, Paul calls some people *dogs*. In chapter 4, he names two people and asks them to settle their disagreements.

Church life is tough. All of us want to give up from time to time. "I am tired of dealing with those people," we have all said at one time or another. We think that we can call it quits at church but keep loving Jesus. I understand that mood.

Yes, other people have given up on Christianity. I have said to myself more than once, "If that is what it means to be a Christian, count me out."

This past week, we remembered the infamous insurrection of January 6, 2021. Standing out in our memory were those capital insurrectionists who carried Bibles and waved the Christian Flag and led in prayer when they took control of the House of Congress. It makes us sick, doesn't it? We want to run as fast as we can in some other direction.

Still others have been unable to manage the swelling doubt in their minds, or balance their faith with their habits and desires, or understand why their prayers are unanswered, why their friends remain sick, and why they do not feel the faith, hope, and love they profess. They finally give up and drive away.

Occasionally, I run into people who say, "Yes, I remember the day I finally quit." You think they might be talking about smoking or working or drinking. But what they mean is, *believing*. They woke up one morning and realized that they no longer believed.

IV.

Paul begins this wonderful ancient letter with these words, "Whenever I pray, I make my requests for all of you with joy" (1:4).

One half of our church theme this year, *Sing for Joy*, picks up one element of this statement. But I want to grab hold of the rest of that sentence, "Whenever I pray, I make my requests for you with great joy."

I pray that your love for God will never dissolve in the acids of organizational tension. I pray that your faith in Jesus Christ will never disappear in the fog of uncertainty. I pray that your joy in the Lord will never be drowned out by the chaos and confusion of life.

You know what else I pray? I pray that your delight in serving the Lord and loving your neighbor and speaking words of hope will never be overshadowed by the darkness of disagreement or the irresponsibility of fools.

I pray that the memories of the hour you first believed will never be lost in the stories of human meanness or the struggles of misunderstanding.

I pray that the day you last believed never comes, that the hour you first believed will grow ever more precious to you, ever more important to your life, ever more central to who you are as a person.

I pray that you will always give thanks that somebody told you about Jesus, that somebody or some book described the love of God in ways that made you want to believe, and trust, and follow.

I pray that you will always be glad that some minister took you into the water of baptism and dipped you all the way under and brought you up dripping wet.

I hope you will always be able to sing …

Through many dangers, toils and snares I have already come,
'Tis grace hath brought me safe thus far,
    and grace will lead me home.
How precious did that grace appear the hour I first believed.

Four

What Really Matters

I want you to understand what really matters.
Philippians 1:10

These are bad days for the faith and practice of Christianity in the United States. There has been a precipitous decline in church membership, allegiance, and attendance.

- Half of the white evangelical community has run off with Donald Trump.
- Catholics are divided for and against Pope Francis.
- The Reformed Church of America formally divided recently, and the United Methodist Church came next. Our own denomination (Cooperative Baptist Fellowship) is itself only 30 years old, having broken away from the Southern Baptist Convention.
- The abuse of money, sex, and power is rampant within the Christian community.
- Many life-long practicing adults are watching their children drift further and further from Jesus Christ.
- Churches are closing every week. Pre-pandemic data tells us that 4,500 churches closed, and only 3,000 new churches

opened. Some estimate that 30% of the churches will close their doors over the next decade.[11]

These are bad days for the faith community that seeks to worship and follow Jesus Christ as Lord.

Here is my question: what really matters? What really matters in your life? What really matters in our little congregation? What really matters in the United States? What really matters in the world? What really matters?

There are many things that can occupy our minds, command our attention, and engage our resources; but what really matters? There is much that appeals to our affections, and some things that can pull us into addiction; but what really matters? This is the question I put to Paul, the apostle, as I read his short letter to the Christians in Philippi.

Paul introduces this phrase: what really matters. I have read and reread this little letter, asking the question, what really matters? I invite you today to ask that question: of yourself, of Paul, the apostle, of our Lord Jesus Christ. Together, we can seek an answer so that we might live pure and blameless lives until "that wonderful day when the glory of our great God and Savior, Jesus Christ, will be revealed" (*Titus* 3:13).

I.

Three themes are woven all the way through this letter, themes that create the pattern that makes this little epistle so delightful, so attractive, and so powerful in our lives. There are other things, other colors, other textures here as well, but these three ideas are on my mind today.

---

[11] Of the many sources, see the reporting of Religion News for March 15, 2022, posted on their website www.religionnews.com.

Prayer is one theme of the letter. Paul repeatedly mentions his own prayer life and calls the Philippians to prayer. Generosity is another theme of this letter. The gospel work of Paul flourished because these believers in Philippi were faithful and generous and cheerful in their giving. Friendships also play an important part in the Philippian drama. Paul was close friends with some who lived there, and he was even closer friends with some he sent there to carry this letter, to report the news, and to deliver back to him their offerings.

These three elements might occupy some place on a spiritual food chart. Those of you who have taught certain subjects in school know there is a food chart: some things at the bottom and some things at the top.

I read a book this week by friend and theologian Curtis Freeman. He directs the Baptist House at Duke Divinity School. He published a little book called *Pilgrim Letters*.[12] It takes Hebrew 6:1 as its starting point, that place where the writer mentions 6 foundational things: repentance, faith, baptism, laying on of hands, resurrection, and eternity. These are things that are confessed, and believed, and taught by everyone, everywhere, and at all times, to quote the famous maxim of St. Vincent of Lerins.

The letter to the Philippians gives scant attention to any of these Christian ideas. They may not rise to the level of what really matters. There is no reference to baptism, or ordination, or Calvinism, or any type of organization. There is no mention of male headship or gay exclusion, of female subordination, or of any kind of heresy.

But we have a clue as to what really matters tucked away in this little book by Dr. Freeman. Dr. Freeman quotes the late, great theologian John Prine! "I look below, I look above, I am surrounded by your boundless love."[13]

---

[12] Minneapolis: Fortress Press, 2021

[13] John Prine (1948-2020) was a popular singer-songwriter in the folk, country, and Americana tradition. He died from the COVID at the age of 73 in April of 2020. It was after his death that I discovered him and came to love his lyrics and music. This quote is from the song "Boundless Love" on his last CD, *The Tree of Forgiveness* (2018). See also

Yes, **love** is an idea that Dr. Freeman pulls into his exposition of Hebrews 6:1. It is also an idea at the very center of our sweet little letter from Paul, the apostle. "God knows how much I love you," he writes in verses 7 and 8 of chapter 1. "You have a special place in my heart." In chapter 2, he writes: "Make me truly happy by loving one another." In chapter 3, he addresses them as "my dear brothers and sisters." In chapter 4, he writes, "I love you and long to see you."

Throughout the letter, Paul mentions their kindness, their concern, their generosity, and their attention to his needs. These are the marks of love. These are the marks of Jesus. In this way, people could tell those first believers had been with Jesus. Jesus said, "Love one another" (*Gospel of John* 13:34).

In answer to a question posed by a seeker, "Of all the commandments, of all the scriptures, of all the obligations of our religion, what matters most?" Jesus said, "Love God and love your neighbor" (*Matthew* 22:34-40). He never mentioned doctrine, or sacraments, or authority, or buildings, or committees, or a person's standing in life and society. "Love God and love one another."

Love is one of three things in this letter about which we can say, "This is what really matters."

How do we love each other? Let us count the ways.

We love when we hear somebody complaining, and we forgive them.

We love when we see somebody struggling, and we come to their assistance.

We love when we give up something precious to us to supply the need of another.

We love when we sing the song they prefer instead of the one we desire.

We love when we defend someone when it would be easy to join in the criticism.

---

my articles about him at themeetinghouse.net/commentaries. See my article in the fall 2022 issue of *Christian Ethics Today* titled "Eating That Gospel Pie: Religious Rhetoric in the Songs of John Prine."

We love when we take food to somebody's house in response to a crisis.

We love when we hold the hand of somebody who is crying.

We love when we seek to understand a person rather than explaining what we think.

We love when we forgive somebody before they even know they have wronged us.

We love when we do for another what we wish they would do for us.

Who has loved you this week?

Maybe the best way to spend our worship hour is to recount the ways somebody has loved us this week. Maybe we need a testimonial time when we give thanks for the way somebody, sometime, this week loved us with a word, a card, a hug, or a gift. Perhaps it was a small kindness, a sweet smile, a forgotten slight, or a forgiven curse.

Who loved you this week? Give thanks to God.

God so loved **you** that God sent Jesus to be your friend, your guide, your inspiration, your teacher, your savior, your risen Lord.

Love is what really matters.

II.

Joy is another thing that really matters. If love is an attitude and an action directed toward one person, joy is a spirit that emanates from your self, your soul, your innermost being out into the world in all directions. I envision it as rays of sunshine going out in every direction, touching every person, and lighting up every square inch of creation. Joy overflows from your spirit into the spirit of everything everywhere.

I chose this short epistle of Paul, the apostle, to read, study, and inspire my preaching because of this theme: Sing for joy. Dance with joy. Work with joy. Share with joy. Speak with joy. Laugh with joy. Pray with all joy.

It is the superstructure of Paul's desire for the Philippians. "Rejoice. Again, I say Rejoice! Be joyful. Count it all joy. You are my joy. Rejoice in the Lord."

Joy is not a matter of intelligence or personality or the circumstances of life. It is a gift of the spirit of Jesus. Jesus was a joyful person: not dour, or sad, or negative, or complaining, or criticizing, or whining, or giving up. To be full of the Spirit is to be full of joy.

I receive a periodic email newsletter from a friend in Virginia. At the bottom of his email, as part of his signature, is the wonderful reminder, *Joy is the most infallible sign of the presence of God.* I like that affirmation. I like to be with joyful people, to sing with joyful people, to work with joyful people.

People have problems, I know. I have problems. You have problems. Even the people on both sides of this letter—sending and receiving—had problems. Paul was in jail! The Philippians were a small, struggling, marginalized group with external opposition and internal dissension. Paul's antidote to those troubles? Joy!!

What brings you joy? What nurtures joy in your life? Many people put music at the top of the list: playing music, singing music, hearing music. Others mention food: preparing food, eating food, sharing food. We don't know much about Jesus and music, but we know that food was at the center of his life and ministry.

Friends were also important to Jesus, who said, "Now you are my friends" (*Gospel of John* 15:15). Paul, in this little letter, writes about his friends: Timothy, Clement, and Epaphroditus. The television sitcom *Cheers* had the best theme song, also about friends:

Sometimes you want to go where everybody knows your name,
And they're always glad you came,
You want to be where you can see our troubles are all the same.
You want to be where everybody knows your name.

What brings me joy? I will name books, and sunshine, and flowers, and victory, and phone calls, and poetry. What brings me joy? Laughter and hearing people laugh. Some of the best videos on the internet are soundtracks of people laughing, especially small children and babies. Laughter is the best medicine. "He who has a merry heart has a continual feast" (*Proverbs* 15:15). This is the only text of scripture that has hung in a frame in my home for decades.

What brings you joy? Cultivate it. Seize it. Treasure it. Make some joy this week. Ask God to give you an extra supply of joy this week, and share it with those around you. Invite the joyful Jesus into the inner recesses of your soul today. Open up your heart and mind and attitude to the holy spirit of joy.

Joyful, joyful, we adore thee, God of glory, lord of life!!

III.

Love is what matters. Joy is what matters. But at the top of the hierarchy of needs and desires, of gifts and graces, is this name: Jesus Christ, the Lord.

That is the central feature of this letter. Fifty-two times Jesus is mentioned by name or by title and many other times by pronoun. Paul mentions Jesus more often than we normally do in an hour of our worship. Jesus was in his heart and on his lips.

"We rely on what Christ Jesus has done for us" (3:3).

"We are slaves of Christ Jesus" (1:1).

"I will continue to be bold for Christ" (1:20).

"Live pure and blameless until the day of Christ's return" (1:10).

"For me, living means living for Christ" (1:21).

"Rejoice in the Lord" (3:1).

"I become righteous through faith in Christ" (3:9).

"I want to know Christ" (3:10).

"God's peace will guard your hearts and minds as you live in Christ Jesus" (4:7).

Paul knew the Scriptures, but Jesus was on his mind. Paul understood the history and the doctrines, but it was Jesus he wrote about. Paul practiced all the habits and rituals of his religion, but it was Jesus Christ the Lord who was in his soul and mind and heart, who was on his lips and in his pen, who dominated his advice and his direction to the Philippians.

I question any religion that is not full of Jesus. I want the version of Christianity that speaks about Jesus Christ, that sings about Jesus, our Lord, that testifies to what Jesus was and is, and that looks to Jesus Christ for inspiration. There are versions of Christianity, both formal and informal, that relegate Jesus to the back room, to second place, to merely illustrative roles in how we live, and move, and have our being. That's not for me.

As a teenager, I heard the call of God on my life: not to be a preacher, or teacher, or pastor, but to be a person, a human, a member of the global family. I heard God say to me, "If you want to be all I have designed for you, be like Jesus, love like Jesus, work like Jesus, speak like Jesus."

"I can do everything through Christ," Paul wrote to us, to me, in this short letter (4:13). "I can do everything through Christ who gives me strength." And I need strength today. This week. This year. Don't you?

IV.

I began this chapter with a litany of loss for the Christian community in the United States. I have read this biblical letter over and over again, asking such questions as: How shall we live? What shall we do? What is it that matters most?

The answer I get, again and again, is not change your worship, or clarify your doctrine, or join a new network, or remove the pews from the sanctuary, or broadcast on Facebook, or adopt any other organizational gimmick.

No, what matters is this: *love the ones you are with.* Love the ones around you, the ones you see day by day: neighbors, children, students, clerks, employees, members, visitors, even strangers.

No, what matters is this: *live with joy, sing for joy,* walk with joy, laugh with joy, pray with joy all the time, in all circumstances, with all people. "Always be full of joy in the Lord. I say it again—rejoice!" (4:4).

No, what matters is this: *Jesus Christ, our Lord,* who was born of the virgin Mary, went about doing good, healed the sick, listened to the confused, fed the hungry, and touched the outcast. It is Jesus, who was crucified and buried after a sham of a trial driven by false witnesses. It is Jesus who suffered for you and for me.

This Jesus, whom God raised from the dead, is the One who forever lives to make intercession for us, who will come again some day to redeem us all and renew the world.

This is Jesus, the one we love, worship, and follow. You belong to the Lord Jesus. We press on, don't we, as Paul wrote, "to possess that perfection for which Christ Jesus first possessed me" (4:13).

Thanks be to God.

Five

Everything That Has Happened

Everything that has happened has helped to spread the Good News.
Philippians 1:12

I am curious about everything that has happened, aren't you? We watch movies, read books, subscribe to magazines, and talk to our friends to find out all that has happened. Perhaps you are like me and want to know about victory and defeat, illness and healing, marriage and divorce, war and peace, friends and enemies, success and failure.

I have followed with great interest the story of two people, a father and daughter. He is a Baptist minister with a Ph.D. who fell into alcohol addiction, entered recovery, and founded a recovery intervention ministry. She is a lawyer who strayed from her Baptist-Christian ways, started therapy, discovered the Rosary, and converted to Catholicism. Where are they now, what are they doing, how are the two narratives intertwined, and can they say, "Everything that has happened has helped spread the Good News"?[14]

---

[14] Rev. Dr. Terry Ellis and Lauren Ellis DeWitt, both of Baton Rouge LA. Listen to my podcasts at TheMeetingHouse.net/podcasts.

I.

What about your life?

What is your narrative? What has happened to you, and has any of it helped spread the Good News? What about our church: can we say that all that has happened--decline, conflict, pandemic, weather--has helped to spread the Good News? I ask the same question about the Christian Community in the United States: what has happened, and has any of it helped to spread Good News?

These are the three circles of curiosity that shape my reading of *Philippians*. Yes, I know that what really matters in the short letter is love for neighbor, joy in difficulty, and Jesus Christ as Lord and Savior. But Paul makes a claim for himself and his life: everything that has happened has helped to spread the Gospel.

Think of the things Paul mentions. He is in jail. How he got there is included in that phrase, "everything that has happened." He abandoned his persecution of Jesus' followers and became one of them. That's part of "everything that has happened." In this letter, he names things that preceded his change of direction: "I was circumcised," he writes in chapter three (and here I paraphrase), "I was a pure-blood Jew, of the tribe of Benjamin. I joined the Pharisees and studied the Bible and obeyed the Bible. I even obeyed the Law, the Torah, without fail, without fault. Then I persecuted the followers of Jesus. All of this pre-Jesus life, all of these things that I now repudiate as worthless have helped to spread the gospel."

What happened in your life before you got serious about Jesus?

Did you learn a skill like playing the guitar? Did you travel to places like Southeast Asia? Did you major in finance or engineering or psychology? Did you fall into addiction or bad company? Did you marry the wrong person or take the wrong job? Did you mismanage a business or mess up a life? What can you list when you describe "everything that has happened"?

I hope you can say, "God has used in surprising ways some of the things I did before I met Jesus." Some of my failures help me to understand people and testify to people and love people. Some of my mistakes have given me empathy with people, have opened up doors of opportunity with certain people, have pushed me in better, healthier, holier directions."

II.

You never know how something that happens to you will be used by God. The movie, "American Underdog," is the story about everything that happened to Curt Warner. Little did he know that his early love for football would lead him to the Super Bowl, the Pro Bowl, and the movie screen. All of that has made an influential and impactful testimony for Christ.

The book, *Unbroken,* is the narrative of everything that happened to Louie Zamperini during World War II and afterwards.[15] His plane crashed in the Pacific. He spent 47 days in a rubber raft with two other survivors. He had no way of knowing, in those pre-Christian days, how this episode would define his life and offer him a compelling platform for testifying for Christ.

Life is full of tough times that later turn into something positive. Jimmy Carter lost his bid for a second term as President of the United States. What a bitter defeat for anybody. Once upon a time, I was voted out as interim pastor, and I recall how disappointing that was!! But for President Carter, that defeat handled with dignity and grace, became part of his story, and his story has helped to spread the Good News. I once sat in his Sunday School class in Plains, Georgia, and listened as he talked about Anwar Sadat and Menachem Begin.

How has everything in your life helped the cause of Jesus Christ?

Has your history, the good, the bad, and the ugly, made you kinder and more compassionate? Has it made you stronger and more

---

[15] Laura Hillenbrand, *Unbroken: A World War II Story of Survival, Resilience, and Redemption* (New York: Random House, 2010). There is also a children's version of the story, with a slightly different title, and a movie (2018).

courageous? Has it given you a word of witness that is more clear and more centered on Jesus, our Lord?

Has everything that has happened to you formed you as a disciple of Jesus, made you a person shaped by mercy, justice, and humility, a person loving God with all your heart, soul, mind, and strength, and loving your neighbor as yourself? Has everything that has happened to you made you more surely a person of prayer, a person of service, a person of faith? Has it made you a person who is *singing with joy and living with hope*?

You never know when learning a language or perfecting a skill or following a dream will position you as a leader among people, as a teacher of people, or as a neighbor to people around you. Every episode of your life can prepare you to be the person God wants you to be!

III.

Sometimes we wonder how the bad things fit into this equation.

Let's turn to everything that happened to Paul, the apostle. In writing to the church at Corinth, he summarizes much that had happened. He had experienced bad stuff, tough stuff, and hard stuff. He never says God sent this stuff. He never says God predestined him to suffer.

Here is the way he writes in what we call the second letter to the Corinthians: "Five times I have received 39 lashes. Three times I was beaten with rods. Once I was stoned...." And he doesn't mean smoking weed! "Three times I was shipwrecked," and we have an extensive account of one of those shipwrecks. "I have been in danger from robbers, from rivers, from Jews and from Gentiles, in the city and in the desert and on the sea. I have been through hardship, through many sleepless nights, in hunger and in thirst, often without food, in cold weather where I was exposed to real danger" (11:24-26 and following).

37

Then he writes this: "The God and Father of the Lord Jesus Christ knows I am not lying."

Sometimes people do lie about what happened. Just last week, a young student had to give up a Rhodes Scholarship to Oxford University because she had claimed things in her life narrative that never happened.

I once supervised a denominational minister assigned to the campus where I served. He was in charge of the students of his denomination. He was, and is, very impressive, and now has a national ministry and a national audience. But I got curious and suspicious of some of the things that he claimed happened to him. I started calling names and places on his resume. I was right. He had fabricated some of it and embellished some of it. I confronted him, and he confessed.

Paul writes to the Corinthians and to us: "God knows I am not lying."

Some people suffer through hard times. Sometimes they are embarrassed and ashamed. Sometimes they keep it quiet. But other times, they share it and ask God to use the hard times and the weak times and even the wrong times for the good news of Jesus.

Paul wrote to the Romans and said, "All things work together for good" (8:28), and we might expand that to assert, "All things work together for the Gospel."

If you are weak, call upon the strength of the Spirit, and live in hope.

If you are in trouble, pray about it, seek the help of others, and live in hope.

If you have failed in business or love or health, accept things as they are, and ask God to show you what to change and how to follow Jesus.

If you are being pushed out of your family, or your circle of friends, or your favorite club, shake the dust off your feet, and find your way to the promised land.

Read these words of the Gospel, and make them your own: Everything that has happened and everything that is happening and everything that will happen can be used by God in your life, in our lives, to draw you to Christ, to draw us to *sing for joy and live with hope.*

Do not complain. Do not take revenge. Do not give up. Do not lose heart. Do not blame others. Do not curse God.

Like Paul, I have been through troubles. Jesus said, "In this life you will have many troubles" (*Gospel of John* 16:33). My family has been through troubles. We have handled just about everything you can imagine. I can make a list like Paul: addiction, divorce, mental illness, depression, accident, poverty, incarceration, adultery, termination, sickness unto death, alienation, homelessness, and loneliness. Some of these we brought on ourselves. Some were the result of the actions or inactions of other people. Some relate to genetics. Some were random, from nowhere, from somewhere.

I'm still *singing for joy and living with hope,* and you can as well. I am still believing the good news and living the good news and preaching the good news. I am believing God that everything that happens can be used by God to expand the kingdom, to spread love, joy, and peace, to establish justice and overturn wickedness, to display the good news: that God created all things, that Jesus Christ died for our sins, and that we can be filled with the Holy Spirit.

I am trusting God that everything that has happened—the events and the memories, the victories and the failures, the good times and the bad times—can be rolled up in the goodness and grace of God. God can wrap it up in love, decorate it with the ribbons of mercy and joy, and present it to the world as a testimony to this: God has begun a good work in us, among us, and through us, and God will complete it, in spite of what happens, so that when Jesus Christ appears, God will be glad. God's work will be done. And we will *sing for joy and live with hope.*

Six

Defending the Good News

I have been appointed to defend the Good News.
Philippians 1:15

Some Wednesday evenings, we gather online for a period of prayer, sharing, and discussion about the sermon from the previous week. This session, which we call "Deeper," always closes with the host reading the scripture text for the coming Sunday. I listened as Lisa Obermiller read this week from *Philippians* chapter 1, verses 15-19. Her reading included this sentence, written by the apostle Paul, "I have been appointed to defend the Good News." This one sentence reached out and grabbed hold of my imagination and my mind. Maybe it will grab your attention as well.

I.

As a pastor, preacher, teacher, and evangelist, I am called upon to describe the Gospel, to declare the Gospel, and to defend the Gospel. I am also to equip you, each of you, to describe this Good News, to share this Good News, and to defend this Good News. The word *gospel* is often translated Good News. When I was a youth, in

1966, the American Bible Society published *Good News for Modern Man*. Even that title was soon out of date, and they renamed it the *Good News Bible*. They still publish that volume, edited and updated many times.[16] This translation pioneered the now popular strategy of translating thought for thought rather than translating word for word. In other words, take any sentence in the Greek language and put it into the best idiom of modern English. It was a strategy for describing the Good News in ways people could understand, in declaring the Good News in a very readable book, and in defending the Good News against those who seek to destroy it, against those who deny the truth and impact of the Good News, and against those who distort the Good News into something that is neither good nor news.

In some places around the world, people are seeking to destroy the religion of those who follow Jesus Christ as Lord. This week, the American non-profit organization Open Doors published its annual list of places in the world where living a Christian life is dangerous. Afghanistan tops that list, with North Korea second. Three hundred sixty million people live in places where it is dangerous to follow Jesus.[17]

Powerful people seek to suppress the faith and practice of The Way because they sense that it threatens the established order in economics, politics, or religion. A long-time friend of mine has spent his life as a missionary among people whose baptism is a death sentence. He has taken a pseudonym, Nik Ripken, in order to protect even himself. His book, *The Insanity of God,* describes all of this. God bless those who defend the Good News in the face of those who seek to destroy it (and them).[18]

---

[16] By some calculations, the *Good News Bible* (in its many iterations over the 50+ year history) is the most widely distributed modern English translation of the Bible. That fact alone makes translator Robert Bratcher the most impactful graduate (1941) of Georgetown College in its almost 200-year history. I had the privilege of meeting Dr. Bratcher more than once. He died in 2010. See also chapter 25, especially note 59.

[17] See their annual list at www.opendoors.org/en-US?persecution/countries.

[18] Nik Ripken with Greg Lewis, *The Insanity of God: A True Story of Faith Resurrected* (Nashville: Lifeway, 2013).

Others must defend the Good News against those who deny it. Recently, a prominent Christian musician, Brady Goodwin of Philadelphia, posted a 24-minute video on his website to renounce his faith. "I sent a letter to my church," he said, "telling them to cancel my membership." He had been a founding member of the contemporary music group The Cross Movement.[19]

Perhaps he had been influenced by a cohort of atheistic writers who formed what is called the New Atheists. They are known as The Four Horsemen of the New Atheism: Richard Dawkins, Christopher Hitchens, Daniel Dennett, and Sam Harris. They have written books with titles like *The End of Faith*, *The God Delusion*, *God is Not Great*, and *Breaking the Spell*.

In every generation, talented writers also take up the task of *defending* the Good News against those who deny the faith and practice of those who follow Jesus as Lord and Savior. We give thanks for theologians like Hans Kung, writers like Rachael Held Evans, and scholars like C. S. Lewis. There are playwrights, poets, even comedians who take up the good work of defending the Gospel against those who attack it. God bless these apologists for their inventive and influential work.

II.

Still others must defend the Good News against those who distort what we believe and how we live. This is what Paul faced as he sat in his prison cell and wrote to the congregation in Philippi. He refers to their enemies: "Don't be intimidated in any way by your enemies" (1:28). He describes those who have false motives in their gospel work: "Those others do not have pure motives as they preach about Christ. They preach with selfish ambition, not sincerely …" (1:17). And he denounces those who substitute religious ceremony for the righteousness that comes by faith: "Watch out for those dogs,

---

[19] Watch the video at youtube.com/watch?v=eXkIOyRitqs.

those people who do evil, those mutilators who say you must be circumcised to be saved" (3:2).

Then and now, people distort the Good News and make it into something it was never meant to be. The Christian rapper had this in mind when he tweeted in 2022, "Once upon a time I thought I was done with Christianity. But the reality was I was just done with the institutional, corporatized, gentrified, politicized, culturally exclusive version of it."[20]

Yes, from the first day until now, people have turned the kingdom of God into something it was never meant to be. Some have retreated to a hideout, a monastery, or a commune, thinking that following Jesus means seclusion from the world. Some have marched into the halls of power, thinking that following Jesus means domination over others. Some have gathered on a hilltop, thinking that following Jesus means ceasing the work and rest of ordinary life because Jesus is returning any day now.

Each of these options takes some legitimate element of our faith and practice and distorts it, twists it, bends it to the breaking point. We must defend our faith against such distortion. We must defend the Good News. "We" means not just me as a preacher, apologist, and evangelist, but also you as a witness to Jesus Christ, our Lord, risen from the dead and alive forever more.

In our day, no distortion is more dangerous than that known as Christian Nationalism. This is the most powerful and consequential religious movement in the United States today. It is driven by this verse in *Genesis*: "So, God created human beings in his [God's] own image. In the image of God, he [God] created them, male and female he [God] created them. Then God blessed them and said, 'Be fruitful and multiply. Fill the earth and have dominion over it'" (1:28f).

The command "have dominion over it" has produced a philosophy called Dominionism. It calls for Christians to take dominion over

---

[20] Lecrae tweeting from @lacrae on January 18, 2022.

all of society, over all of culture, over all our common life in these United States. In fact, Christian Nationalists have identified what they call "7 mountains of cultural power." Take control of these 7 mountains, they claim, and we will control the United States. Take control of these 7 mountains, and we will make the United States a Christian nation. Take control of these 7 mountains, and, at last, we will be all that God predestined us to be.[21]

These "7 mountains" are family, business, government, art/ entertainment, education, media, and religion.

These Dominionists are, in reality, distortionists. These distortionists take over the family and impose male domination over female. These distortionists take over education, one school board after another. These distortionists take over religion, one denomination or one congregation at a time. These distortionists take over government, one legislature at a time, and one justice at a time.

This is the way to evangelize America, these Dominionists contend. This is the way to a create a national community as Jesus envisioned it. This is the way to obey the command of Jesus to be his witnesses in Jerusalem, Judea, and Samaria. The surest sign of the fullness of the Spirit is to take over everything of importance. That is their distortion of the faith and practice of Christianity. They believe this is what Jesus meant when he said, "Come, follow me!" Or so they say!

III.

What do *you* think? Does this sound like your religion? Does this describe what you embraced when you said Yes to Jesus? Does this feel like the way Jesus calls you to live and move and have your being?

---

[21] See, for instance, Lance Wallnau, Bill Johnson. *Invading Babylon: The 7 Mountain Mandate.* Destiny Image Publishers, 2013.

Like Paul, the apostle, we must defend the Good News against this distortion.

After reading the book, *The Power Worshippers,*[22] by investigative journalist Katherine Stewart, I wrote to her. The book is a history of the rise of Christian nationalism, beginning 70 years ago. It is a description of the agenda of Christian nationalism, taking over congregations, denominations, school boards, legislatures, and a national political party.

I asked her, "Is there a version of Christian faith and practice that is strong enough, organized enough, and courageous enough to push back against Christian Nationalism and offer a compelling alternative to their version of Christianity?"

She wrote back these sobering words: "The religious movements of the left are mainly theological movements, while the religious movements on the right, Christian Nationalism, are political movements."[23]

Her concern is our concern: people claiming the name of Jesus who distort the faith and practice of Christianity. This is why thousands, even millions of people are quitting church, giving up on Christianity, even turning away from Jesus. They are saying, "If that—Christian Nationalism—is what it means to be a Christian, count me out."

They see Christian nationalists leading the mob that stormed the capital one year ago, and they are disgusted. We are disgusted. They hear Christian nationalists twist religious freedom into the right to discriminate against anybody who does not believe like they do and vote like they do, and they are discouraged. We are discouraged. They listen as Christian Nationalists use religious rhetoric to undermine the basic elements of democracy, education, and freedom, and they are angry. We need to be angry.

---

[22] Katherine Stewart, *The Power Worshippers: Inside the Dangerous Rise of Religious Nationalism* (New York: Bloomsbury, 2019).
[23] Email, Katherine Stewart to Dwight A. Moody, January 23, 2022

Like the apostle Paul writing to these Philippians, we need to repudiate these who distort the gospel message of Jesus, those who long for the return of white Christian America, and those who deny the rights of women, minorities, and immigrants, in favor of their own preferred status—all in the name of Jesus.

We need to offer our own testimony: "This ain't right!"

This is not the way to follow Jesus and worship God and love our neighbor. This is not the Good News that people everywhere need to hear. There is nothing good in it. It is bad news for the country and for the church of Jesus Christ, for you and me and all our neighbors.

IV.

"Conduct yourselves in a manner worthy of the Good News," the old apostle wrote to those new believers (1:27). "Live as children of God, shining like bright lights in a world full of crooked and perverse people," he wrote to them a little later in this letter (2:14). And when he wrote earlier "to understand what really matters" (1:10), I listed those three things as love for one another, joy in every circumstance, and a constant focus on Jesus Christ as Lord and Savior.

This is our best defense of the Good News: *to sing with joy and live with hope.*

Yes, some defend the Gospel through intellectual arguments and theological explanations. I have been powerfully influenced by such people, like C.S. Lewis. His *Mere Christianity* has sold millions of copies because it is a clean and clear argument for the truth of the Good News. Others defend the Gospel through organizational arguments. They point out the history of good works of Christian hospitals, orphanages, schools, and global non-profits, like the Church World Service, the Lutheran World Relief, and our own Global Missions Offering.

But the most powerful way to describe the Good News, declare the Good News, and defend the Good News is through your life, a life well-lived, a life patterned after Jesus of Nazareth. "Let this mind be in you that was also in Jesus Christ," Paul writes (2:5), introducing that early Christian hymn. It is a life shaped by that grand trilogy of Micah the prophet: "Do justice, love mercy, and walk humbly with God" (*Micah* 6:8).

C. S. Lewis himself, among the greatest of modern intellectual defenders of the faith, wrote this: "When we Christians behave badly, or fail to behave well, we are making Christianity unbelievable to the outside world."[24]

When Christians squabble, the world is listening. When Christians act with lust or pride or prejudice, the world is watching. When Christians are more interested in our own rights and privileges, the world points a finger and accuses us of failure to live the Gospel.

A life of beauty and kindness and courage is the best defense of the Gospel. You be that person, starting today. To fill the world with love and grace and mercy is the best defense of the Good News. Let us do that today. To speak the winsome word of forgiveness to the fallen and the word of welcome to the stranger is to be the very presence of Jesus for somebody today. You can do it and do it with flair.

To *sing with joy and live with hope* is to declare the Gospel and defend the Gospel, all in one motion. Let's do it. Let's set aside our irritations and prejudices and sing for joy. Let's walk through our disappointments and disagreements and live with hope. Let's forget our preferences and our needs and put on Jesus Christ. Let's do it today and every day!

---

[24] I found this quote in an online search on the site quotefancy.com. It was attributed to Lewis but gave no primary source. I probably should not trust such sources and should not even be including it in a book or a sermon. But it may be an accurate citation of the great writer. Nevertheless, this is fair warning to the reader!

Seven

To Live Is Christ

For to me, living means living for Christ.
Philippians 1:21

Paul has a fistful of famous sayings.

To the Corinthians, he wrote, "These three things will last forever—faith, hope and love—and the greatest of these is love" (*First Corinthians* 13:13). To the Romans, he wrote, "I am convinced that nothing can ever separate us from God's love. Neither death nor life, neither angels nor demons, neither our fears for today nor our worries about tomorrow—not even the powers of hell can separate us from God's love... that is revealed in Christ Jesus" (8:38ff). To the Galatians he wrote, "There is no longer Jew or Greek, slave or free, male and female. For you all are one in Christ Jesus" (3:28).

In this little epistle to the Philippians, consider these:

"You must have the same attitude that Christ Jesus had" (2:5).

"Always be full of joy in the Lord. I say it again—rejoice!" (4:4).

"I can do everything through Christ who gives me strength" (4:13).

These are worthy of the attention they receive, and they certainly are worthy of a sermon once a year. But to this collection, we can add this one: "For to me, living means living for Christ, and dying is even better" (1:21[25]). This short verse calls us to consider our purpose in life, our reason for being, why we are here, and what we must be or do to hear those words on the great Judgment Day, "You done good!"

I.

These dozen words speak to us today. They invite us to say, "For to me, to live, is …. what?"

Paul says, to live is Christ Jesus. This we can understand. He was single and never mentions a thing about a family (although *Acts of the Apostles* does in 23:16). Paul was a convert through a personal appearance of Jesus, the Risen Lord. Few, very few, people have had such a gift. If Jesus himself appears to you and tells you what to do, it would be easier to sum it up like Paul did.

There is one more thing: Paul was convinced that the end of the world was imminent. He mentions the return of Jesus at least three times in this epistle, once saying, "I am convinced that God who began a good work in you will complete it so that it is finished on the day when Christ Jesus returns" (1:6). He says elsewhere, "We are eagerly waiting for Jesus to return as our savior" (3:20). Toward the end of the letter, he writes simply, "Remember: the Lord is coming soon!" (4:5). That last statement would have the effect of clarifying things. It is like being in a building when it catches fire—suddenly, you have one and only one goal in life—to get out, alive.

These three elements of Paul's situation make his clarity, his certainty, and his conviction easy to understand but also hard to relate to. We have families. We have no appearance of Jesus himself. We are not so convinced that the end of the age is just around the corner.

---

[25] Here, I am using the wording of the New Living Translation, as is the preferred text throughout this book; but elsewhere in this chapter (including the chapter title), I resort to the wording of the more familiar King James Version: "To Live is Christ."

But, we also want to feel down in our bones that we are being the person God created us to be, that we are doing what God put us on earth to do, and that we are living out our calling from the Lord Jesus Christ.

II.

Some people dismiss the idea of worshipping God and following Jesus. There is no God, they think and say. There is no God to call you to do anything or be anything. If there is a God, what makes you think God cares about you, knows about you, or has a purpose for your life?

Many people feel like this, think like this, and speak like this. But consider this: Researchers have been reporting for years that the community of atheists worldwide is shrinking, and the communities of believers are expanding. Religious faith around the world has remained strong and vibrant.[26] People are searching for purpose, for meaning, for significance.

We also look into the night sky, as the ancient psalmist did. We see the stars and galaxies, the black holes, and the great expanse of emptiness. We also ask, "What is it all about? Who are we?"

Something in the human spirit keeps bubbling up, keeps poking through the doubt, the skepticism, and the mystery of it all to ask questions: "Why are we here? What is the meaning of it all? Where is it all going? What is life all about?"

We gather each Sunday to worship God, to celebrate the resurrection of Jesus from the dead, and to testify to this: There is in us a Spirit stirring around. There is a longing in us that wants

---

[26] There is much debate about this. The decline of religious affiliation and attendance in the United States has received a great deal of popular and scholarly attention. Some of this decline is shared by other organizations and activities and may be related to the world-wide pandemic. On the other hand, some of the political tension in the world is connected to religious faith and practice, and here I think of religious nationalism in a Jewish country like Israel, in Muslim countries like Egypt and Iran, and in Christian countries like Brazil, Ukraine, and the United States.

to know. There is a voice in us that calls out to us from the deepest places of our being, from the far edges of the universe, and from the highest heaven. There is a presence, a power, a person. We want to know more. We want to feel more. We want to live more. We want to live with more purpose, more clarity, more significance, and more impact.

It is not more power we want, or more money, or even more happiness. We want to live like Jesus Christ, knowing our values, our purpose, and our mission.

We want to be able to say: to me, to live is Christ!

III.

A few years ago, mission statements were all the rage. Corporations and organizations paid consultants hundreds of thousands of dollars to help craft a simple, comprehensive, and compelling statement.

What is our business? What are our values? What is our chief product? What impact do we want to have? JetBlue purports "to inspire humanity, both in the air and on the ground." Tesla wants "to accelerate the world's transition to sustainable energy." TED desires to "spread ideas."

I like that last one. It is just two words. It is very similar to the one-word mission statement of Paul, the great apostle: Christ!

Churches also got into the mission statement act. For several years, this was the focus of church retreats and conferences. Last year, our congregation spent some time searching for a slogan that will summarize our aspirations. We came up with *Sing for Joy and Live with Hope.* I like it very much. It is a kind of mission statement. It is a brand. We have put it on cards. I hope we have put it in our hearts and in our habits.

Even families and individuals joined the pursuit of a mission statement. One family I read about worked together to create their mission statement: "In the Andrews family, our mission is to arise each day with grateful hearts and smiling faces, determined to glorify, serve and trust in God. We live by the highest standards of moral character and integrity. We love, respect, encourage and defend each other. And we're noble stewards of the resources entrusted to us."

Whether you are young or old, a mission statement might be a powerful and practical strategy for you and your family. Perhaps a mission statement is something that will inspire your extended family, or perhaps it is something you can bequeath to your children and grandchildren.

Here are some helpful questions to ask as you create your own mission statement. What is important? Where do I want to go? What does "the best" look like for me? How do I want to act? What kind of legacy do I want to leave behind?

Most mission statements are between one and three sentences, never exceeding 100 words. The best mission statements are typically a single, succinct sentence, so keep this in mind when crafting yours. But I still like the brevity of that itinerant missionary, Paul, who said simply: Christ! To me, to live…is Christ!

IV.

Some people live their entire lives without purpose, meaning, or motivation. This emptiness often dissolves into desperation, despair, and utter defeat. People feel worthless and hopeless. They contemplate suicide. Even seemingly successful people can go down this road.

Elijah, the great prophet of God, was overcome with despair. He gave up his public ministry and retreated to a cave. It is the sign and symbol of many who followed in his steps. Retreat into a cave. Cut off communication. Ignore friends. Dwell on the loss or defeat or hurt.

Just before the 2022 Winter Olympics, people mourned the loss of Australian skier Brittany George. She was only 24 years old.

The aspiring Olympian was found dead in a Brisbane neighborhood in Queensland, Australia, on January 27. In a podcast prior to her untimely death, she described her mental and emotional state: "It has literally been my whole life. I've been 'the athlete' from when I was 2 until when I was 20 or 21," she said. "I did not have an identity. I was labeled 'the athlete' from a very young age and just rode with it... I put everything in. My injuries [and] my schoolwork went second-hand, everything went second-hand to sport...It was absolutely all or nothing. You're an athlete but who am I? Who am I as a person? Who is Brittany? I don't know that...I struggle every day to know who that is."[27]

Some people are like Brittany: to me, to live is sports, the NBA, the Olympics. To me, to live is music: singing, performing, even achieving fame and fortune. The Voice!! You might have to confess: to me, to live is family, my children, my grandchildren. Everything I do is for my family. Some people dedicate themselves to a cause, like freeing the slaves or saving the planet. Others dedicate themselves to an organization, even the church!

Many of these mission statements or life ambitions come from a good place deep inside of us, a place full of love and compassion, a place overflowing with justice and peace.

The mission statement of Paul gathers up all the good stuff inside of us, all of the best intentions and noble desires, all of our human obligations and Christian expectations and synthesizes them into a single word—Christ.

To me, to live is Christ: to live in Christ, so that my destiny is bound up with Jesus Christ. Where Christ is, I am. Where Christ goes, I go. What Christ is, I am. This is our confidence, that God binds your life with the life of Jesus. God raised Jesus from the dead, and God will raise you. God prepared a place for Jesus, and God prepares a place for you.

---

[27] This podcast conversation is sad and sobering. https://youtu.be/oS4E7Xmz3r8

I also want to say, "To me, to live is Christ and to live for Christ." My purpose in life is like that of Christ. I want to love God and love my neighbor: the neighbor who lives in the house with me and the neighbor who flees their homeland to find refuge in my neighborhood. I want to live, full of the spirit of Christ: full of compassion in a time of need and courage in a time of trouble. I want to live in the spirit of Christ, to live with justice, mercy, and humility.

Paul wrote in another place that to be full of the spirit, the spirit of Jesus, the Christ, is to be overflowing with love, joy, and peace, with patience, kindness and goodness, and always with faithfulness, gentleness and self-control (*Galatians* 5:22 KJV). That is what it means to say: "For to me, to live is Christ!"

Eight

Citizens of Heaven

Above all, you must live as citizens of heaven.
Philippians 1:27

In May of 1974, my wife Jan and I boarded an El Al flight in Tel Aviv and headed home. We had lived in Jerusalem since the summer of 1973. During that year, we studied the history, explored the land, and gathered for worship with a wide and wonderful assortment of people.

It was a non-stop flight, some 14 hours, as I recall. It was the end of the most formative experience of my adult life. I remember flying into New York and catching a glimpse, for the first time, of the grand lady of American aspirations, the Statue of Liberty. "I lift my lamp beside the golden door," the poet Emma Lazarus wrote. A surge of adrenaline shot through my soul, and tears welled up in my eyes. I was glad to be home. I was glad this is my home.

What did the poet write? "Breathes there the man, with soul so dead, who never to himself hath said, 'This is my own, my native land'?"[28]

I am proud to be an American. I was glad to get home to the United States. Since then, I have traveled to Europe, Africa, and

---

[28] Sir Walter Scott (1771-1832), "Breathes there the man."

South America. But every time I returned, I saw and felt with the Scottish poet, "This is my own, my native land."

I.

Paul had some of this patriotic emotion in him. In *Philippians*, he describes his Jewish identity. From start to finish, from beginning to end, Paul—or Saul, to use his given name—was a Jew, born in Tarsus in modern day Turkey. He moved to Jerusalem, studied Torah, and pursued the way of the Pharisees, then the most Bible-focused, law-abiding of all the ways of being a Jew.

Paul had earlier claimed his Roman citizenship. You recall the story (from chapter 16 of the *Acts of the Apostles*). Paul and Silas were arrested for disturbing the peace in Philippi. They were stripped and beaten and thrown into jail, into the inner dungeon, the text says. The next morning, the magistrates sent word for them to be released. But do you recall what Paul said? "No way! They beat us and threw us into jail without a trial. We are Roman citizens. So now they want us to leave secretly? No way! You tell those magistrates to come here personally and make amends" (16:37, paraphrased, of course!).

Paul was aware of his Jewish heritage, and he embraced his rights as a Roman. He also traveled much of the known world: Judea and Arabia, Asia and Greece, the islands of the Mediterranean, and the capital city of Rome. He was, in many ways, a citizen of the world.

But he had a deeper, wider connection with Jesus. He was, he proudly claimed, a citizen of heaven. It was this passport that he treasured most; it was this loyalty that shaped his soul and determined his decisions.

He wrote to the churches of Ephesus: "You are no longer strangers and aliens, but you are fellow citizens with the saints" (2:19). He wrote to these Philippians asserting, "We are citizens of heaven" (1:27).

Just as the Ukrainian conflict was reaching its peak, our congregation had two guests. One is a Mexican native, the other a Russian native. Both met in the United States and became citizens. Today, they work in Kyiv, Ukraine. Between them, they carry 4 passports. They speak at least 4 languages. They are citizens of the world, and I admire them greatly.[29]

We need more of that spirit, that connection, that wide-angled way to view the world in our little church. We want to be deeply loyal to our town, to our county, and to our state. But we want to be global citizens, alert to what is happening in the world, alarmed at the dangers and dramas in all directions, and engaged through both prayer and action for the redemption of the world and the renewal of all things. I want to be a member of a church with a global vision, a global ministry, and a global membership.

II.

About that same time, early in 2022, the pastor of the Global Vision Bible Church near Nashville gathered his people under a large revival-style tent and said this: "I've got the first and last names of 6 witches that are in our church. You were sent to destroy us. And you know what's strange, 3 of you are in this room right now."[30]

That pastor is deranged, in my opinion. That kind of nonsense is one reason people are giving up on church, on Jesus, and on God. I repudiate it entirely. But I like the name of the church: Global Vision Bible Church. Yes, I know that often a Bible Church is the most conservative, fundamentalist congregation in the county.

---

[29] Mina and Gennady Podgaisky are field worders for the Cooperative Baptist Fellowship, assigned to Kiev, Ukraine. They departed Ukraine shortly before the war began and took up residence in Black Mountain, North Carolina. They spoke to Providence Church shortly after the war began and also during the early weeks of our journey through this *Epistle to the Philippians.*

[30] There are many media reports of this episode. See, for instance, www.independent. co.uk for 15 February, 2022.

I often wonder if such people have read the Bible, the whole Bible. The Bible is a radical book, a transformative book, and a book that upends our values and our behaviors. It challenges our presuppositions and our prejudices. It calls us to repent, change our ways, and live according to the values of heaven.

People in Tennessee, Texas, and elsewhere are banning books they consider dangerous, books that challenge their social norms, books that poke fun at our prejudiced, self-centered ways. The book they need to ban, according to those criteria, is the Bible. This book has a radical vision of behavior, of belief, and of belonging.

"There is a wideness in God's mercy," is the way one hymn writer puts it, even as churches all around us sing a different chorus: "There is a narrowness to God's Gospel, there is a smallness to God's circle, there is a tightness to God's truth."

I grew up in a long-standing church culture that told the "colored folk" to sit in the balcony and behave, that told the "women folk" to sit in the pews and be silent, and that told the "gay folk" to sit in the closet and stay there. Too often, that is what it means to be in a "Bible Church."

There is a radio broadcast entitled "Back to the Bible." This media ministry is based in Lincoln, Nebraska. For years, it featured the teaching and preaching of the late, great Warren Wiersbe (whom I liked very much, having met him at a conference somewhere). That title is premised upon the notion that we have strayed from the Bible, and we need to get back to it. What they mean, it seems, is: we have grown too liberal, too secular, too inclusive, too ecumenical—we must get *back to the Bible,* they say, with its tight hold on who is in and who is out; *back to the Bible,* they say, with its narrow way of loving God and loving each other; *back to the Bible,* they say, with its closed circle keeping the few in and the many out. That's what they mean by *back to the Bible,* and that is what is implied by the name "Bible Church."

A teacher of mine many years ago said, "The Bible is so far ahead of us."[31] We must spend our lives trying to move forward into the world it envisions, into the community it describes, into the citizenship, the heavenly citizenship, it promises.

The Promised Land is ahead of us, not behind us. Beloved Community is ahead of us, not behind us. The Kingdom of God is ahead of us, not behind us. We need to go forward, not backward.

Jesus is ahead of us, not behind us. "Follow me," Jesus said, accurately describing where he is and where we are. Jesus is leading us out of the darkness of our prejudice, out of the deepness of our self-deception, and out of the narrowness of our understanding.

Paul was a Jew. Paul was a Roman. But Paul was a citizen of heaven. It was that citizenship that made him famous, successful, controversial, influential, memorable. It was that citizenship that got him arrested, beaten, jailed, and eventually martyred.

Paul floated above his ethnic identity and saw its limitations, its hostilities, and its prejudices. "I once persecuted Jesus and those who followed in the Way," he confessed. "I was full of devout energy and certainty." But he pushed side all of these things. Here, he famously writes, "I once thought these things were valuable, but now I consider them worthless...." (3:7).

He also rose above his Roman identity. He knew and shared the Roman values of law and order, of authority and administration, of safety and security, and of travel and trade. His loyalty, however, was not to Rome, but to the Righteous Lord of heaven and earth, Jesus Christ, the One who was compromised by Jewish friends and crucified by Roman soldiers but raised from the dead by the God of all eternity.

God raised Jesus from the dead. That is the Good News.

---

[31] Dr. Clyde Francisco of the Southern Baptist Theological Seminary in Louisville, where I studied from 1974 to 1982.

III.

Rome has come and gone, but Jesus is still Lord of heaven and earth, of time and eternity. Jews are still here, a respected and dignified people; but in Christ, there is neither Jew nor Greek, neither slave nor free, neither male nor female, neither gay nor straight, neither rich nor poor, neither black nor white…just people, just humans, just children of God, just citizens of heaven.

For many years, our American citizenship and our church membership told us that black people were second class and needed to work the fields, sit in the back of the bus, and stay out of our church. But our heavenly citizenship tells us that we were blind to the truth and deaf to the Gospel. We did wrong century after century, and we are still doing wrong.

Some people still do not think Black Lives Matter. They do not think we need to teach about our despicable history regarding race. Some have not repented of our past and do not want the past brought up in the present. But our heavenly citizenship demands that we right some wrongs, mend our ways, and speak the truth. I am often ashamed to be a Southerner, but I am never ashamed of the Gospel that calls me, in the words of this little letter from Paul, "to stand together with one spirit and one purpose, fighting together for the faith, which is the Good News" (1:27).

I am a citizen of heaven.

Mary Alice Birdwhistell was a freshman at Georgetown College when she stood to speak one Saturday morning. I was serving as dean of the chapel and professor of religion and sitting on the front row of that chapel. I was astonished at her poise, her skill, her articulate message to a chapel full of potential college students and their parents. Later, in private, I said to her some version of this message, "Have you ever thought about preaching?" She looked shocked and said something like, "My church would never permit that." She spoke for many in our day and for most in the history of Christianity.

We have told the women, in the words of the song, "sit down, sit down, sit down, sit down, sit down you're rocking the boat." The church pushed a deformed vision of community life upon the whole country: women could not vote, or fight, or judge, or serve, or minister, or preach. They were second class citizens, we told them, and in so doing we were denying our own status as citizens of heaven (not to mention preventing many from hearing the good Gospel word).

We were hiding our heavenly passports and pulling out earthly passports that declare our membership in what Paul calls, "a world full of crooked and perverse people" (2:15). The apostle called us, instead, to be "bright lights" in a dark world. We were hiding our light under bushels of prejudice and power.

I'm glad to say that young woman is now senior pastor of Highland Baptist Church, Louisville, Kentucky, with degrees from Georgetown College, Baylor University, and Truett Seminary.

The gospel heritage of our own wonderful little church includes three women who served as our pastors. I honor them all: Gail Coulter, Julie Merritt Lee, and Mary Apicella. I give thanks for each one.

Calling out their names reminds me of the overlooked comment buried right there in the story of Paul returning from his missionary travels: "The next day we went on to Caesarea and stayed in the home of Philip the evangelist, one of the 7 original deacons. He had 4 daughters who have the gift of prophecy" (*Acts of the Apostles* 21:9). His 4 daughters were prophets, preachers, and proclaimers of the word and way of God!

Did you ever hear a sermon on that verse of scripture?

Thank God, we are beginning to live according to the ways and means of our heavenly citizenship. Paul writes: "I pray that you will keep on growing in knowledge and understanding" (1:9). This is what is happening in the church today—we are growing in knowledge and understanding of the Gospel.

IV.

Did you ever hear a sermon or join a study on this part of scripture?

This is what the Lord says,
Be just and fair to all. Do what is right and good.
For I am coming to redeem you
 and to display my righteousness among you.
Don't let foreigners committed to the Lord say,
 "The Lord God of Israel will never let me
 be a part of God's people."
Don't let the eunuchs say,
 "I am a dried up tree with no children and no future."
I will give them—within the walls of my house—
 a memorial and a name ...
I will bless the foreigners who commit themselves
 to the Lord....
I will bring others, also, besides my people, Israel.
 (Isaiah 56:1-8)

This expansive vision of inclusion is the Good News of God. Religious people long ago were drawing a circle that shut many out, including both foreigners and those unable to have children. But God drew a circle that took them in.

Isaiah the prophet, however, was seeing into the future; he was seeing the Beloved Community, the Kingdom of God, that heavenly citizenship. The prophet heard the Gospel invitation: "No, come on in. There is room for you. There is room for all. God loves you and so do I, and Jesus died for all of us."

This book of Isaiah is what lay open on the lap of the Ethiopian diplomat as he traveled home from Jerusalem. The story is told in chapter 8, verses 26-40 of *Acts of the Apostles*. An angel told Philip to travel a certain road and approach a certain man. Philip "met the treasurer of Ethiopia, a eunuch of great authority under the Kandake [Candace], queen of Ethiopia. The eunuch had gone to Jerusalem to worship. and he was now returning. Seated in his carriage, he was reading aloud from the book of the prophet Isaiah."

He was reading from *Isaiah* chapter 53, verse 8, these words: "Unjustly condemned, he was led away. No one cared that he died without descendants, that his life was cut short in midstream."

About whom was he talking, the Ethiopian asked Philip?

And I ask, why was he fixated on this text?

That Ethiopian eunuch, like the eunuch in chapter 56 of *Isaiah* and like the man described in Isaiah 53 who was killed without justice and without children, was a man excluded from the people of God because he could not have children. He represented a demographic different from the norm, from the majority, unable to produce descendants, and thus living outside the circle. Today, he might be grouped into that demographic we know as LGBTQ. According to Gallup, Inc., this demographic comprises 7.1% of the American population, by self-selection.

LGBTQ are a misunderstood, misjudged, and mistreated minority. In the religious communities of both Old and New Testaments, of Hebrew and Christian faith, they have been misunderstood, misjudged, and mistreated. We drew a circle and shut them out. God drew a circle and drew them in. That is the Gospel, the good news.

Can I ask the questions of Paul (from *Philippians* 2:1-2)? "Is there any encouragement from belonging to Christ? Is there any comfort from the love of God? Is there any fellowship together in the spirit? Are your hearts tender and compassionate?"

Paul responds to these rhetorical questions with his own request. "Then make me (Paul and me, your pastor) truly happy by agreeing wholeheartedly with each other, loving one another, and working together with one mind and purpose," and I add, "regardless of race, color, gender, or sexual orientation."[32]

"May the grace of the Lord Jesus Christ be with your spirit" (4:23).

---

[32] In January of 2023, Providence Church adopted the following statement of policy: "Providence Baptist Church is a congregation open to the imagination of the Holy Spirit which relationally affirms God's love within the complex mosaic of all human diversity. In all facets of the life and ministry of our church, including but not limited to membership, baptism, ordination, marriage, teaching, and committee/organizational leadership, Providence Baptist Church will not discriminate based on race, gender, sexual orientation, gender identity, gender expression, ethnicity, marital status, age, physical or mental ability, economic circumstances or place of origin."

Nine

Questions of the Soul

*Is there any encouragement from belonging to
Christ? Any comfort from his love?
Any fellowship together in the Spirit? Are your
hearts tender and compassionate?*
Philippians 2:1

Encouragement. Comfort. Fellowship. Compassion: Which of these
do you need today?

These gifts are in short supply. We have too much discouragement,
too often discomfort, too little fellowship, and way too little
compassion. Paul, the great apostle, asks his Philippian friends four
questions: Is there any encouragement? …. any comfort? …. any
fellowship? ….. any compassion? He needed all of them, as do we.
He was in jail, perhaps in Rome, with an uncertain future and few
friends. He wrote, "We are in this struggle together" (1:30).

That's the way we feel, isn't it? We are in this struggle together,
while dodging the COVID, enduring the divisions in the country,
and praying that things don't explode into another insurrection
or even outright war. We are trying to stay in touch with friends
and family: some isolated and some on a political tangent that has
separated them from us. We are trying to pay bills, raise our children

and grandchildren, and make a good life for ourselves. Now, we are watching Russia invade Ukraine and wondering if all of Europe could slide into war. "The sun is going down," John Prine sings in a song about his father's sudden death, "and the moon is just holding its breath."[33] That speaks to me.

This ancient letter can speak to you and me today. These four questions about encouragement, comfort, fellowship, and compassion bring us this answer: one way to keep us joyful and hopeful in the trying circumstances of life is to have a spiritual fellowship with people of faith. Paul himself wanted what we want: encouragement in knowing and serving Jesus Christ, comfort by living in the love of God, fellowship with others through the joy of the Holy Spirit, and compassion for others and from others who also want to flourish as people, as a family, and as a community, as a country, and as a global family.

This is what Paul wanted. This is what I want. Is this what you want?

I.

Let's look closely at these four questions Paul writes for us in the letter to those early Christians.

First, note that the Bible is full of questions: in the stories, in the psalms, in the gospels, and in the letters. Which of the questions in the Bible come to your mind? Here are some of the most famous. "Who can separate us from the love of God?" Paul wrote to the Christians in Rome (*Romans* 8:35 KJV). "Where is he born king of the Jews?" asked the wise men from the East looking for the newborn Jesus (*Matthew* 2:2 KJV). "Am I my brother's keeper?" is the famous question Cain asked God, after he had killed his brother Abel (*Genesis* 4:9 KJV).

---

[33] Again John Prine, whom I came to appreciate shortly after his death in 2020. This song is called "Mexican Home." See note 13 above.

There are approximately 2,550 questions in the Bible. I know; I counted. Today, I am using what I call my Question Bible, with every question underlined or marked.[34]

The "question" is one of the most interesting and compelling elements of human communication. Your mind automatically stops to answer when a question is asked, even random questions, irrelevant questions, insulting questions, and serious questions. I am tempted to give a sampling of the questions from Jerry Seinfeld, or John Prine, or *The Narnia Chronicles*. You could also offer some questions of your own, I am sure.

In *Philippians*, we have four questions. They are the only questions in this short letter. But the letter itself generates some questions. Was Paul released from jail? Did he ever return to Philippi? Why are the two Philippi episodes described in *Acts of the Apostles* not mentioned in this letter? Did the two women he urged to settle their differences ever make amends? Who were the "enemies" Paul writes about? Who are those people he describes as "those in Caesar's household"?

There are other questions: How can we be content in all circumstances? How can we do all things in Christ who strengthens us? How, like Paul, can we rejoice in all circumstances?

These are good questions, don't you think?

II.

I have many questions about my own about life, and love, and loss. I am sure you have questions about your life.

---

[34] Years ago, when I first became intrigued with questions as an avenue for understanding and revelation, I read through the Bible—a New Revised Standard Version—and noted every use of the question mark, writing at the bottom of each page the number of question marks on that page. I know such punctuation marks are not in original manuscripts and are therefore a matter of translation and interpretation. My counting is, at best, an estimate; but I think it is a very good estimate!

For instance, I wonder about mental illness: where it comes from, what triggers it, how to treat it, and how to endure it?

I wonder about our country. How did people get so angry, and what do they want and why? Why do people want to distribute guns and ban books? Will democracy survive? Why do we tolerate gerrymandering? How can we encourage people to vote? Why are the political parties so polarized? Isn't there a great deal we agree on? Can we work together and solve our common problems?

I wonder if I can keep up with the technology. This week, I tried to learn a new program. My engineer said to me when I spoke of my frustration, "You need to get your grandson Sam to help you!" He is 15 years old.

What is coming down the technology pike to help us or hurt us? Will it make most of what we know obsolete? I'm just trying to learn how to change the channels on my smart TV. I have YouTube TV, but I don't know much about it. How much change or progress or disruption can we handle?

I wonder why I married the person I did, took the job I did, and made the friends I did. I wonder how I got here. I wonder where I will be next.

What will happen to this church? Will we survive our struggle? What will happen to the Christian Community in America? It is declining so rapidly. People are jumping ship so often that there can't be much room left in the water. In another 20 years, will there be a church like ours, or organs like ours, or buildings like this, or full-time professional ministers like me, or people like you sitting in pews, listening to sermons and lifting hands in prayer?

I wonder.

In mulling these questions, I am in good company with God, Jesus, and the Spirit. This book of God and this story of Jesus are full of questions.

Does God know all the answers? Does God know all the questions?

I come again to these questions in *Philippians*: Does belonging to Christ provide any encouragement? Does knowing the love of God provide any comfort in this life? Does living in the fullness of the Spirit bring any fellowship to me, to you, to us, to them? Is there among us, in this church, in this congregation, enough tenderness and compassion to help us navigate life and celebrate life, to help us forgive each other and serve each other and show compassion to those we meet?

These are the questions Paul penned in this letter. They are the questions that confront us today.

Can we find answers? Can the search for answers itself be a journey to wholeness and holiness, to happiness, to redemption? Can asking these questions of the soul be the way of salvation?

III.

The Gospel has a few answers but rarely to the questions we ask. One great answer, though, is our need for the community of joy and hope: singing our souls into harmony with God and one another; praying our way through trials and tribulations; reading our way into the grand story of God, Jesus, and the renewal of all things; forgiving anyone and everyone as God, in Christ, has forgiven us; and seeing in each other our common humanity and our shared salvation, so that we can say with the great imprisoned apostle, "I can do everything through Christ who gives me strength," but ... but that depends upon a lot of help from you! (*Philippians* 2:13f, partially paraphrased!)

That is our aspiration as a congregation. There are four ways we are leaning into the church we want to be. The first is music. I am so glad our church has a long history of singing with a choir. What is better than a choir? What is better than singing? The Gospel commands us to "be filled with the Holy Spirit, singing psalms, hymns, and spiritual songs among yourselves" (*Ephesians* 5:18-19).

Did you notice that? We are speaking to one another as we sing! Yes, we sing for ourselves, and yes, we sing in praise to God, but yes, we also sing for our neighbor.

I remember sitting next to my father in church and listening to him sing. He could not read music or carry a tune. But the words and the spirit were coming from his soul, his heart, his innermost being. It made a real impression on me.

When you are discouraged, we sing for you. When you are defeated, we sing for you. When you are down and out, somebody needs to sing "Bridge Over Troubled Water."

A second way we are becoming the church we want to be relates to food. You know the best part of the church week? It is not the choir, not the prayer, and not the sermon, but the food! Each Sunday, we go out to eat together. Last week, there were 18 of us in the sanctuary, and 12 went out to eat. Four others were still a little nervous about the COVID. But two thirds of the congregation gathered around a long table, lifted our bread in praise, and laughed and talked and carried on. That is the Lord's Supper.

Jesus was the man who ate with saints and sinners, and there were plenty of both gathered around that public table last week. I don't know who is a saint and who was a sinner. And I don't care. But nothing binds our souls and lives together like the communion that follows the worship service. Where are we going to eat today?

Third, I want to mention service. Later today, some of you will gather at our Providence House to distribute food and comfort, drink and conversation with those who need it. You dispense the supplies we all have contributed: socks and blankets, soup and sandwiches, toothpaste and soap, and gifts of the Spirit. In the background, I hear the sound of that old gospel song:

> *Mercy there was great, and grace was free.*
> *Pardon there was multiplied to me.*
> *There my burdened soul found liberty.*

I contend that the worship meal at Providence House is as close to Calvary as we will ever get. For a decade and more, it has been the place for answering the questions: Is there any encouragement for anybody? Is there any comfort for those whose lives are uncomfortable? Is there any fellowship across racial lines, ideological divides, or social stratification? Yes, it is in the fellowship of Jesus.

Finally, I name hospitality. This week, I have the distinct honor of speaking to the monthly gathering of PFLAG. It is the local chapter of the national organization of Parents and Friends of Lesbians and Gays. This local chapter was birthed here in our church, and for many years this was their home. When one of their members heard that I was the scheduled speaker, he wrote to me:

> *There are 180 Baptist churches in Henderson County. 179 of them are either Southern Baptist or independent fundamentalist, and the nicest thing that I can say about 179 of them is "bless your heart." Providence is different. It is that one Baptist out of 180 that sings a different song. You sing a song that says queer folks are loved and accepted by God. You sing a song that one can be Baptist and call out Christian Nationalism. Every other year, PFLAG HENDERSONVILLE conducts a study about LGBTQ youth homelessness. In the most recent survey, 50 young adults participated, and 30 of them indicated that they experienced faith-based homelessness. 22 of these folks were kicked out of non-affirming Baptist churches. ...... I want my community to hear your Baptist hymn. I want my community to know that there is a Baptist church that is singing a song of joy where people who are different can sing together.*[35]

---

[35] This email message came to me on February 24, 2022, from Joshua Bledsoe and is used by permission (stated in an email on August 12, 2022). PFLAG of Hendersonville was birthed in Providence Church and continued to meet in the church building for many years.

That is just another way of answering the questions: Does belonging to Christ provide any encouragement? Does knowing the love of God provide any comfort in this life? Does living in the fullness of the Spirit bring any fellowship to me, to you, to us, to them? Is there among us, in this church, in this congregation, enough tenderness and compassion to help us navigate life, to help us forgive each other, and to help us show compassion to those we meet?

I say, yes! Hell, yes! And thanks be to God!

Ten

This Same Attitude

You must have the same attitude that Christ Jesus had.
Philippians 2:5

The Russian invasion of Ukraine is a perfect counterpoint to the great hymn to Christ, which Paul inserted into this brief letter. The invasion of a neighboring country by the tanks, planes, ships, and soldiers is evidence of the worldly lust for power by that barnyard rooster named Vladimir Putin.

How different is the spirit and substance of our Lord Jesus Christ!

The hymn in *Philippians* chapter two says it well (and I paraphrase): he had it all, but gave it up for you, for me, and for the world. He relinquished his power, renounced his crown, and became a servant, a slave. He died for us, and with us, and in our place.

This man, Jesus, is the true servant of God. No wonder Paul, the transformed apostle, could preface this hymn, not with the name of its composer and not with today's preferred tune, but with this simple admonition: that attitude of Jesus, let it be in you and me, as well.

This same attitude that made Jesus such a servant and savior is the attitude that will make you all that God wants you to be. It will make our church both the people of God and a blessing to the world.

I.

Some of you are waiting for my reference to John Prine. Many a sermon from this preacher is incomplete if it does not quote the lyrics of a John Prine song. I am glad that my tenure here has introduced some of you to the late, great songwriter. But I must tell you: I could claim today's inspiration from Paul, the apostle. Long before preachers integrated poems and lyrics into our presentation of the Gospel, Paul had already done it.

My teacher, the famous and influential Dale Moody, notes in his book of systematic theology the 12 hymns that comprise *First John* and the ten hymns that are included in the pastoral epistles (*First Timothy, Second Timothy,* and *Titus*).[36] He quotes the short hymn of those early believers that many years ago the Apostle Paul embedded in the *Ephesians*: "Awake, O sleeper, rise up from the dead, and Christ will give you light" (5:14).

With our hymns, we praise God: "Holy, Holy, Holy, Lord God Almighty, early in the morning our song shall rise to thee!" With our songs, we pray to God. We sang such a prayer on Ash Wednesday. "Have thine own way, Lord, have thine own way." With lyrics set to music we teach what we believe: "In Christ alone my hope is found. He is my light, my strength, my song." With a hymn, we will call each other to the communion table this morning, "Let us break bread together on our knees." We should not be surprised that Paul

---

[36] Dale Moody (1915-1992) taught Christian theology for 44 years. His book, *The Word of Truth: Summary of Christian Doctrine Based on Biblical Revelation* (Grand Rapids: Eerdmans, 1981), remains a valuable asset in understanding Christian things. See especially the entry "hymns" in the index. Dale Moody is no relation to me, but we were close friends; he supervised my dissertation and preached my ordination.

also uses poems, lyrics, and hymn texts to express his understanding of the Gospel.

We come now in this letter to the Christians in Philippi, to the most famous of all the early Christian hymns. It describes the life of Jesus, our Savior, in 3 movements:

1) Christ was with God from the beginning;
2) Jesus humbled himself and took up human life; and
3) God raised Jesus Christ from the dead and placed him above all creation.

This is the Gospel. The son of God was with God in creation and redemption. The son of God was born in a stable and laid in the manger. As a baby, he was given the name Jesus. As an adult, he inaugurated the kingdom of God. After evil men killed Jesus, God raised him from the dead. This story line is what we celebrate through the Christian year: Advent, Christmas, Lent, Easter, and Pentecost.

This is our story. This is God's story. This is your story.

II.

Paul quotes this hymn, but he introduces it with this simple directive: you must have this same attitude. Perhaps he was saying an ancient version of "You need an attitude adjustment."

Attitude is what is in your mind, your heart, your soul. It is what we feel deep down. It is the wellspring of all that we do. We can suppress it for a while. We can cover it up in the short term. We can deny how we feel. But in the end, our attitude will come out.

That is why Putin is such a good public example of what not to be. He has spent 30 years cultivating the world, building economic ties with nations, and shaking hands with presidents. But his actions reveal that deep down, his motives were clearly fake. He was always scheming, plotting, and planning to do what he has done to exert his power and disrupt the peace. Like a banty rooster, he is strutting across the world stage. He thinks he's somebody. But he is a nobody, a rude, crude, and totally unacceptable nobody. His behavior is that of a strutting rooster: "Look at me! Ain't I somebody?" But he's a nobody, a violent, despicable nobody.

Putin grasped for that which he did not have. Putin is seizing that which belongs to another. Putin wants to be high and lifted up, but by his actions, he has shown himself to be low down and dirty. Putin is the opposite of Jesus.

The hymn in *Philippians* says that though Jesus was in the form of God, though he was in the heavenly places with God, though he was the agent of all creation, he did not think this equality with God was something that he needed to clutch. Instead, Jesus gave up his divine privileges.

Elsewhere, the Bible tells us not to "think you are better than you really are" (*Romans* 12:3). Some people do. We say they are egotistical. We say they are self-centered. We say they are narcissistic. All they think about is themselves. All they want is attention. All they do is put themselves forward.

Mark tells a story in his gospel account of Jesus (10:35ff). "James and John, the sons of Zebedee, came over and spoke to Jesus. 'Teacher, we want you to do us a favor…. When you sit on your glorious throne, we want to sit in places of honor next to you, one on the right and the other on the left.'"

Their friendship with Jesus had gone to their heads. Jesus was a celebrity. He drew crowds wherever he went. He, no doubt, had both a Twitter account and personal bodyguards. These two disciples wanted the status of Jesus. They wanted the attention of the people. They wanted to be seen. They needed an attitude adjustment, didn't they?

Remember, these were two of the Twelve, two who traveled with Jesus, two who were given authority and responsibility, and two who were leaders in the church. How easy it is for even church leaders to let their status and influence go to their heads, to want the attention that belongs only to Jesus, to strive to be the stars. This attitude is a danger to everyone and everything. It is a contradiction of the Gospel of Jesus, who had everything and gave it up that he might be the servant of all.

The story continues: "Jesus responded to them, 'You don't know what you are asking!'" When the other disciples heard what James and John had asked, they were indignant. Jesus called them together for a little talk!

Jesus had to deal with jealousy and envy and bad attitudes right among his important and influential disciples. That makes us feel better, doesn't it? We Christians look around our congregations sometimes and despair. There is too much tension, too much opposition, too much irritation, too much ambition, and too much ego. Sadly, this is the way it often is because we are just people, with all the possibilities and problems that are common to humanity.

"Jesus called them together and said, 'You know that the rulers of this world lord it over their people, and officials flaunt their authority over those under them. But among you it will be different. Whoever wants to be a leader among you must be your servant and whoever wants to be first among you must be the slave of everyone else'" (*Matthew* 20:25-28).

Read those words again: "The rulers of this world, the economic, political, and religious leaders of this world lord it over their people." Look up that verse on Google and you might just see a picture of Vladimir Putin. He is the antithesis of Jesus. Putin is, in that sense, the anti-christ; but there are many who exhibit the opposite of Jesus, the opposite of what we are called to exhibit. There are many anti-christs, and some are in the church.

III.

It is his Christ-like attitude that inspires so many people to love and admire Jimmy Carter. He was a peanut farmer from Plains, Georgia. He was elected governor of Georgia. In 1976, our bicentennial year, he was elected President of the United States.

It was a hard four years. We remember it as a time of the oil embargo, high inflation, and the Iranian hostage crisis. These things crushed his presidency. Jimmy Carter lost his re-election bid. With humility and grace, he conceded defeat and moved on with his life. He has never lost his sense of self, his humility, his Christ-like spirit.

I invoke Mr. Carter as an illustration because, like us, he is a Baptist-style Christian, dipped all the way under and brought up dripping wet. Like us, he is affiliated with the Cooperative Baptist Fellowship.

Jimmy Carter has been the best ex-President the country has ever had. He has traveled the world, building houses with Habitat for Humanity and advocating for fairness in elections. I have toured the Carter Center in Atlanta and worshipped at the Maranatha Baptist Church in Plains, Georgia. One of my former students, Jeremy Shoulta, was, for a time, Mr. Carter's pastor at Maranatha Baptist Church in Plains, Georgia.

I went to hear Mr. Carter speak once. It was at a gathering of Baptist people, and Mr. Carter was advertised as the featured speaker. But I was late that morning, as I have often been, even to church gatherings, weddings, and funerals. When the funeral directors in Owensboro, Kentucky, referred to me as "the late Dr. Moody," this is what they had in mind.

That morning, I was directed to the back of the room and seated at an empty table. A welcome was given, and the blessing over the meal was said. Our food was served, and I ate alone. Suddenly, the door at the back of the room opened. It was perhaps 15 feet from me. Four people walked into the room. Jimmy Carter, Rosalyn Carter, and two Secret Service agents. Jimmy Carter walked straight up to me, extended his hand, and said, "Hello, I'm Jimmy Carter."

I should have said, "I know who you are!" But I said, "I am Dwight Moody." He said, "That is a famous name." I said, "I have a famous name, but you are a famous person."

He spoke to others around me; he took a seat at the table next to me at the back of the room, away from all the dignitaries, among the people who were late to breakfast. How like Jimmy! How like Jesus! How like we are called to be: content with a seat at the back of the room.

"Have this mind in you," Paul wrote in this letter to the Philippians (2:5), "which was in Christ Jesus." As you do justice, and love mercy, you can also walk humbly with God and with each other.

Have this attitude!

Eleven

Dying with Hope

Jesus gave up his divine privileges.
He took the humble position of a slave and
was born as a human being.
He humbled himself in obedience to God and
died a criminal's death on a cross.
Philippians 2:7-8

The Gateway Arch on the St. Louis riverfront opened in June of 1967. A few months earlier, my family had moved to that great city, and it was there I finished high school.[37] I recall my first ride up one side of that arch and down the other. They call it the Gateway to the West. It is 630 feet high, the tallest monument in the world. It is the same distance from one base to the other: 630 feet. Those dimensions form a parabola. Engineers know it by a more technical name, a catenary. It is the form created by a chain hanging from both ends, reversed.

I recall vividly the day the late William E. Hull came to St. Louis and preached a sermon on the prologue to the *Gospel of John*. He held up a silver chain, like you might use for a necklace or with a pocket watch. He held it at each end, allowing the chain to fall

---

[37] Hazelwood High School, Florissant, Missouri, class of 1968.

80

naturally. He described the shape the chain makes, which scholars call the parabola or catenary. Dr. Hull used its shape to illustrate the gospel message. It was 1971, and I was a college student home for the summer and working in a Coca Cola bottling plant. I was a member of the International Distillers Union, preparing to be a minister!

Etched in my memory is the visual of Dr. Hull holding aloft both ends of that silver chain, one end representing the glory from which our Lord came, the other end representing the glory into which he ascended, and the bottom of that swag, that gospel parabola, representing the great reality we celebrate at Christmas.

"And while they were there, the time came for her baby to be born. She gave birth to her firstborn son. She wrapped him snugly in strips of cloth and laid him in a manger...." (*Luke* 2:6-7).

We call it the Incarnation, a word meaning "in the flesh."

I.

This silver chain, this gospel catenary, this biblical parabola is also the outline of this three-stanza hymn embedded in the *Philippians*. Those early Christians wrote hymns and sang hymns. They, like us, found it easier to remember the story and describe the doctrine if it is situated in a song. Set it to music, and we will sing the Gospel! No doubt, they, like us, had more music memorized than scripture!

Here, then, is the hymn, paraphrased:

Equality with God through all eternity, stanza 1;
Identity with us through the birth, stanza 2; and
Elevation to the place of highest honor, stanza 3.

Theologians will talk about the pre-existence of Christ, the existence of Jesus, and the post-existence of Jesus Christ.[38] I like this outline; I find it compelling. But today, I want to talk about that middle stanza: Jesus humbled himself in obedience to God and died as a criminal, as a servant, and as a person. He died abandoned by the crowd, betrayed by a disciple, and denied by his friends. He died too young, alone, and in pain.

I hope you do not die that way. I hope I do not die that way.

I think of the nine people killed in Texas, when a 13-year-old-boy drove a pick-up truck into an on-coming van full of college athletes on a two-lane road west of Lubbock, Texas. I think of the mothers and babies, lying dead on the streets in Ukraine. I think of the young adults, dying every day of drug overdoses or those who died in a hospital, stricken by the COVID, leaving life with their families waving from the street. I hope I do not die in these awful ways.

But I hope we, like Jesus, can die with hope!

When our time comes, whether by disease or disaster, we can enter the valley of the shadow of death, strengthened by the same hope that prepared Jesus to enter Jerusalem on Palm Sunday, the same hope that enabled Jesus to kneel in the garden on Maundy Thursday, and the same hope that strengthened Jesus to carry his cross to a hill called Calvary on Good Friday.[39]

That is the spirit of hope I want when I come to the end of my days. That is the spirit of hope you need when you face the river that separates this life from the next. We want to live with hope, and we want to die with hope.

---

[38] Dale Moody, *The Word of Truth: A Summary of Christian Doctrine Based on Biblical Revelation* (Grand Rapids: Eerdmans, 1981), pp. 386-408.

[39] According to the *Gospel of John* (27:32), Jesus carried his own cross. In the gospels of Matthew, Mark, and Luke (called the Synoptic Gospels), Simon of Cyrene was forced to carry the cross for Jesus.

II.

Jesus had hope. Jesus lived with hope. He had no guarantee about things. When he stood up in his hometown synagogue, read from the Isaiah scroll, and declared that the prophetic word was being fulfilled that day, he had no guarantee that the people would hear him or believe him or follow him; but he had hope. They ran him out of town and accused him of blasphemy.

When Jesus selected, from among his many disciples, 12 men to be chief among equals, he had no guarantee that those men would stay with him, learn his message, and devote themselves to Gospel work; but he had hope. Most of them did, and what they did fulfilled his best hope.

When Jesus stopped under the sycamore tree and looked up at Zacchaeus and said, "Come on down, I want to go to your house today," he had no guarantee that the little man would actually invite him, hear him, and turn from his wicked ways; but he had hope. By the grace and power of God, salvation came to that house that day! (*Luke* 19:1-10, paraphrased)

When Jesus stood at the tomb of his friend Lazarus who had been dead for 3 days and called out to him, "Lazarus, come out!" he had no guarantee of anything; but he had hope! To the shock of everyone there, Lazarus, the dead man, heard the voice of Jesus, the living man, and that voice stirred him, awakened him, and resuscitated him; and everyone said, "Glory to God!" (*Gospel of John* 11:1-44).

Jesus knelt in the garden of Gethsemane just hours before he was betrayed and prayed that everything he sensed was about to happen might not happen. He had no guarantee that God would hear his prayer and spare him the suffering. He had no guarantee, but he had hope. Judas came and betrayed him, and the soldiers came and arrested him, and the authorities heard his case and condemned him. When he started walking to the place of his execution, he had no guarantee of anything: that his dying would be avoided, that his pain would be mild, or that his death would be for something. He had no guarantee that he had life beyond the grave, but he had hope.

Jesus hoped in God. Jesus put his trust in God. Jesus, our Lord and Savior faced his own death, faced all the mystery that lies beyond, and looked into the unknown world that touches our world in a million thin places. Jesus faced all of that, not with any divine guarantees, but with hope. Jesus lived all his life with hope. Jesus entered death with that same hope.

III.

You also can live with hope. You can die with hope. The gospel hymn puts it this way:

Our hope is built on nothing less
*   than Jesus' blood [death] and righteousness;*
We dare not trust the sweetest frame
*   but wholly lean on Jesus' name.*
On Christ the solid rock we stand,
*   all other ground is sinking sand,*
*   all other ground is sinking sand.*

Geographic metaphors are powerful today: solid ground and sinking sand in the hymn quoted above; and, in another popular hymn, the journey through this land to another land.

Then let our songs abound, let every tear be dry.
We are marching through Emmanuel's land
*   to fairer worlds on high.*

You can march with confidence. You can *sing with joy and live with hope* because we are marching with Jesus and singing with Jesus and living with Jesus.

But may I turn to an image of the engineer and the mathematician? It is not my natural habitat, but, here today, it offers us a way to look hopefully at the end of this life and the beginning of another life.

Our hope in the future is like a graph, like a series of coordinates mapped out on a universal map. One by one, these x-y coordinates are brought to our attention. You recall when you heard God's voice and hurried to the altar and to the baptismal water. Put that on the map.

You remember the songs that stirred your heart as a youth and called you to follow Jesus. Put that dot on the map of life.

You tell the story of how God picked you up after you had failed, how God brought into your life just the right person to love you and support you, how God reached down and protected you in that accident or illness and gave you another decade or two to live, and how God touched your soul and roused you out of bed today and brought you to this sanctuary or to this broadcast and warmed your heart with love and thanksgiving.

Put all these life episodes on the graph. Connect all those dots.

Look around you at the beautiful flowers poking their way out of the cold, cold ground. Observe the simple kindness of people around you and the courage of people we see on the television screen. Take those x coordinates and y coordinates, and add them to this map of God's grace.

Connect the dots. Connect them with a bold line running all through your life.

Which way is that line headed? Extrapolate it off this graph of life into a map of eternity. Where does it point you? Where does that line lead?

I will tell you where it leads—to the love of God, to the grace and mercy of the Lord Jesus Christ, to the strength and peace and joy that are flowing around you and in you, and through you by the Holy Spirit of the living God.

I will tell you where it leads—to the Jesus of Nazareth, who died for you, and to the God of eternity, who raised Jesus from the dead.

I will tell you where it leads—on from this good earth and all its loves and losses, its successes and failures, and its kindness and courage to that bright day where there is no darkness, disease, or death. It leads to that good place where we will lay down our sword and shield and study war no more. It leads to where the lamb will lie down by the lion. It leads to where the river of life flows from the throne of God, and on both sides of that river grows the tree of life whose leaves will be for the healing of the nations (from *Revelation* 22)..

I will tell you where it leads—it leads home.

That is my hope. Is that your hope?

Today I am living with hope. Soon I will be dying with hope.

That will be alright with me.

Twelve

Place of Highest Honor

*Therefore, God elevated him to the place of highest honor
and gave him the name above all other names.*
Philippians 2:9

Many people have watched the YouTube video of the Ukrainian choir singing in a subway station on February 24, 2022. It was the first day of the invasion. The language of the hymn is lost on us, but the spirit, the devotion, and the courage of their singing spread around the globe.[40]

It reminds me of those second-century Christians in Asia, as described by the Roman official known as Pliny the Younger. He wrote to the Roman emperor, asking for assistance in conducting trials for Christians accused of seditious acts. His is the first pagan description of a Christian gathering, and it reads as follows: "They gather before dawn on the first day of the week to sing hymns to Christ as if he were a God, to make a pledge to avoid certain behaviors, and to eat together an ordinary meal."[41]

---

[40] Watch the video at https://youtu.be/L2WsP6FrrDI
[41] Pliny the Younger was the Roman governor of provinces now in modern day Turkey. He wrote to the emperor Trajan around 112 AD (or CE). The letter is known as *Epistulae* X.96 and can be found in many compendiums of early Christian literary sources.

Perhaps their song was the hymn we read in *Philippians*. It celebrates the earthly life of Jesus, it remembers his death on the cross, and it rejoices in the resurrection and all that follows. It describes Jesus crucified, buried, and raised from the dead. It celebrates Jesus receiving "the place of highest honor."

I.

The people who worship God and follow Jesus are singing people. "I sing because I'm happy," the old hymn says. "I sing because I'm free." Ethel Waters sang this song in the Billy Graham evangelistic meetings decades ago.

The Word commands us to "be filled with the Holy Spirit, singing psalms and hymns and spiritual songs among ourselves, making music to the Lord in your hearts. And give thanks for everything to God the Father in the name of our Lord Jesus Christ" (*Ephesians* 5:19).

Sing for joy and live with hope, we say here at Providence. This spirit of thanksgiving and joy is what inspires our music: composition, arrangement, rehearsal, presentation, and remembering. When we gather, it is the most important element of our worship. In singing, we praise God, we elucidate what we believe, we confess our sins, we tell the story of Jesus, we celebrate the wonders of creation, we anticipate the glory of the coming kingdom, and we offer ourselves as living sacrifices. As the old gospel song says, "All to Jesus I surrender, all to him I freely give."

This is why we sing. It lifts our spirits. It confesses our faith. It invites our neighbor to trust God, love Jesus, and open up to the filling of the Holy Spirit. This is also why Paul sang his hymns and why these hymns came to mind as he was writing to the Philippians.

When Paul first went to Philippi, trouble ensued. He was tossed into jail. What did he do there? He lifted his voice in song! At midnight, he and Silas were singing. Maybe they were singing this song. Maybe that is why he quoted it in this letter to those believers in Philippi. In Philippi, in Rome, in Hendersonville, even in Kyiv, we hum some version of the song I learned as a child,

Come we that love the Lord and let our joys be known.
Join in a song with sweet accord,
Join in a song with sweet accord,
And thus surround the throne.

II.

This song, in chapter 2 of *Philippians*, outlines the most important part of our Christian faith: the life, death, and resurrection of Jesus.

Yes, there are many other things we believe and celebrate:

"In the beginning God created the heavens and the earth." The whole Bible begins with one of the most famous opening lines in world literature (*Genesis* 1:1).

When the Hebrew people were slaves in Egypt, God brought them out "with a strong right arm" (*Exodus* 6:6).

God sent the Hebrew prophets to shape the moral life of the people: "to do what is right, to love mercy, and to walk humbly with God" (*Micah* 6:8).

The Bible itself closes with an expansive vision of the coming of God and the renewal of all things. It is pictured as a city coming down out of heaven. From the center of the city flows a river, the river of life. On each side of the river are the trees of life, whose leaves are for the healing of the nations (*Revelation* 22:1-2).

This promise of a coming kingdom helps us live with hope and sing for joy. It is the blessed hope that picks us up when things look bad, when friends die, when wars commence, or when we fall or fail in public or private ways. We are carried along by the river of hope that flows within us and through us.

This biblical song reminds us that at the center of our hope is the life, death, and resurrection of Jesus. Jesus lived. Jesus died for us. God raised Jesus from the dead. These things I believe. This is the core of Christian confession from the very beginning. When those early Christians said, "Jesus is Lord," they meant that Jesus lived among them as he went about doing good, that Jesus died on the cross for their sins and in their place, and that on the third day, God raised him from the dead.

This is also the essence of our belief. This is the content of our preaching and teaching. This is the story we sing and tell and teach. This is the victory we have in Jesus. Any confessing, singing, and preaching that strays from this are no longer Christian confessing, Christian singing, or Christian preaching.

That early song reminds us that Jesus gave up his status in the heavens to take up residence here on earth. He healed the sick. He challenged those in authority. He coached his disciples on how to pray and share and love. Jesus lived a simple life and trusted in God as the One who loved him and provided for him. He gave food to those who needed it and answered the questions of those who came to see him. He wrestled with his own sense of calling. He invited others, including us, to live like he did and prepare for the coming rule of God.

Verse 2 in the hymn Paul embedded in his letter describes how Jesus gave up his own life and died a criminal's death on a cross. This is what Christians remember and celebrate on Good Friday. The religious authorities resisted Jesus and his popular movement. They heard him challenge the temple complex and its version of the godly life. They feared his success and denounced his mission. They conspired with the political authorities, the Romans, to push him off the public stage. They worked a deal with Judas, arrested Jesus on trumped-up charges, and had him lodged in the city jail. They condemned him to torture and death. Jesus died with nails in his hands and hope in his heart.

Verse 3 continues: Therefore, God "elevated him to the place of highest honor and gave him a name above all other names, that at the name of Jesus, every knee should bow, and every tongue confess that Jesus is Lord."

It is this phrase, "the place of highest honor" that grabs my attention today. Where is this place of highest honor?

III.

Where is this place of highest honor? What is this place of highest honor?

Recently, baseball celebrated the career of Jackie Robinson. Seventy-five years ago, Jackie was the first person of color to play professional baseball in the big leagues. It was a big deal, and Major League Baseball made it a big deal. Every major league professional baseball player wore Robinson's jersey number, 42. A street in New York City was renamed in his honor. Statues were unveiled, stories were told, and achievements were celebrated.

Jackie Robinson played ten years for the Brooklyn Dodgers. Then he retired. He died in 1972. We honor him and give him a name that is near the top of those who shaped baseball.

Sometimes we think of Jesus as retired, don't we? He worked for 33 years. He did good, took care of his mother, made friends with a whole troupe of people, and stood for righteousness. He died, a condemned and disgraced man. But God raised him into retirement, we sometimes think. He has a nice home, even a throne. He no longer has to trudge this earth, weather the storms, respond to all the demands on his time, or explain to slow-witted people the true meaning of the Hebrew Bible. He is up there, with God, waiting for the right time to swoop down in glory, bonk all the wicked on their everlasting foreheads, and set up the kingdom of God.[42]

---

[42] It is only fair to explain that some biblical references to "the kingdom of God" and "the kingdom of heaven" refer to life in history, on planet earth, where we live, and other

That's the picture we get, right?

We are waiting for the return of Jesus! The clouds will part, and the Son of Man will descend with a shout. We debate whether it is a two-step process: first, snatching all the saved people out in an event some call the Rapture, and later, sweeping all the lost people into eternal damnation. We are in a waiting period now. Jesus is up there on his heavenly throne, waiting for the judgment day.

The place of highest honor is that throne, in heaven, next to God, right?

Have we not learned anything? Have we not listened to Jesus? Did we not pay attention to Jesus when he was explaining about the place of honor and the place of service? Weren't we watching when he took the towel, the bowl, and the water, and stooped to wash the feet of his disciples? Weren't we listening when he said that the greatest among you must be your servant?

Don't we remember that he was born, not in a castle or a palace or a place safe and secure and worthy of designation as a national monument? He was born in a stable, a barn, a stall. Have you been near a stall lately?

Where is this place of highest honor? Where did Jesus go when the angels rolled that stone away? Where was Jesus that morning when, on the third day, "he got up," as they say in the black church?

Here is what happened: Jesus got up and went back to work!

Jesus got up on that first Easter morning and looked around. He saw the women scrounging for something to eat. He saw the sick, desperate for a cure. He saw the ignorance and superstition of the crowds. He saw how the institutions of his day were more concerned about their own survival than they were about justice, and mercy, and humility.

---

references refer to that which is to come in some distant future, when Jesus returns, and God makes all things new. It can be quite confusing, but it also can demonstrate that perhaps during those first decades of Christian faith and practice, Christian people had different ideas of how to understand the meaning of this very important idea and hope.

Jesus got up and looked around and said, to himself, "There is still a lot of work to do." Jesus got up and went back to work in the barrios of Buenos Aires and the refugee camps of Syria. Jesus got up and went to work on the border that separates Russia from Ukraine and along the river that divides Mexico from the United States. Jesus got up on that first day of the week and went back to work, in the penitentiary in Lewisburg, Pennsylvania, and in the food stamp office in Seattle, Washington.

Jesus is not sitting in some celestial easy chair, counting down the days until he can zap a billion or two and hobnob with a million or two. In the kingdom of God, that does not describe the place of highest honor. That is the mind and imagination of a worldly person, unredeemed and ill informed. That is not the way of God; it is the way of this world.

Jesus got up and went back to work.

I will tell you where Jesus is today. He is serving food this afternoon at the Sunday worship meal on Oakland Street in Hendersonville. Jesus is huddled at the monthly PFLAG meeting, trying to find safe places for the kids kicked out of their homes while they are searching for themselves.

I'll tell you where else Jesus is today. He is at the United Nations, whispering into the ear of ambassadors from everywhere the ways and means of Shalom. Jesus is in board rooms, and bank lobbies, and school halls, and storefront rescue missions.

Today, Jesus is already sitting at the restaurant, waiting for us to finish with our religious business and join him for what we will surely call holy communion. Jesus is sitting in your house, at your kitchen table, drinking coffee while you describe to him the hellish mess that has swallowed up your family. Jesus is sitting on the back row of this small sanctuary, hoping we will celebrate Easter by helping somebody else find a light for their darkness, a cure for their depression, a friend for their loneliness, a hope for their despair, a song for their soul, and a savior for the worst of their lostness.

Jesus wants us to think less about what the Risen Savior can do for us and more about what we can do for those around us. Jesus wants us to bring a little redemption into the life of some person who is today seeking a salvation.

Maybe that person is you.

Thirteen

The Pleasure of God

*God is working in you, giving you the desire
and the power to do what pleases God.*
Philippians 2:13

The song by the late Leonard Cohen, *Hallelujah*, is both popular and puzzling. It has stirring sounds but odd lyrics. The opening stanza has something instructive and useful for us today. Michael Sebastian, our musical genius, will help me with at least the chords, and then Paul, the imprisoned pastor, will help us with the lyrics.

*Now I've heard there was a secret chord
That David played, and it pleased the Lord.
But you don't really care for music, do ya?
It goes like this, the fourth, the fifth
The minor fall, the major lift.
The baffled king composing "Hallelujah."*

I learned something today about the major, the fourth, the fifth, the minor fall, and the major lift. But there is a line that intrigues me: "It pleased the Lord." Cohen alludes to the biblical stories of David: how his spirit from an early age pleased the Lord; how his music later pleased King Saul; how his leadership of the nation pleased the people. "A man after God's own heart" is the way the Bible describes David (*First Samuel* 13:14).

Another central person in the biblical narrative is said to have pleased God. You recall that Jesus, as he was coming up out of the baptismal water, heard the voice of God saying, "This is my dearly loved son, who brings me great joy" (*Matthew* 3:17).

I am sure there are others, men and women, boys and girls, who pleased the Lord. Each of them may help us understand what the great apostle meant when he wrote to the Philippians and to us, that God has put within us both the desire and the ability to please God.

I.

The desire to please is a good news-bad news pressure. We want to please our parents, our teachers, our coaches, and our supervisors. We want to please our spouse, our partner, and our friends. This is not a bad desire. It helps us learn what they want us to learn, do what is good for our own selves, and be all that we can be. To please the Lord may be the ultimate motivation. Isn't that a good thing?

There is a downside to this desire to please.

I recently attended a Baptist meeting in Raleigh. I saw an old friend there, a pastor, and I asked, "How are you? You and your church seem to have fared well during the pandemic." He replied, "It has not been easy. You know me. I am a people pleaser. I tried to please everybody. Too often in these contentious times I was able to please no one." Different ideas about the pandemic and the mask and even public meetings themselves made it difficult to please everyone. Those who tried went crazy!

At other times, pleasing people will get you into trouble. Peers can pressure you to say things and do things that are not right. Adults, as often as teenagers, get into trouble when they do something just because the tribe or club or group is doing it. Somebody this week spoke to me about the Enron affair when scores of people, religious people, Christian people, went along with a scheme to defraud. Giving in to peer pressure is what happened the day Ahmaud Aubrey was murdered in Brunswick, Georgia. That is also what happened at the Capitol, on January 6, in Washington, D.C.

Knowing whom to please and how to please are part of growing up, growing true, and growing wise. David pleased his father, and the king, and the Lord. But later, he got into trouble because he wanted to please himself and perhaps others. In fact, David started life right as a young boy and young man, but later in life, he fell away. He started strong and ended weak.

Moses was the opposite. Moses pleased no one early in life. He had to flee his family and friends. He took up herding on the far side of the mountain, and it was there God found him. But getting old helped Moses please the Lord. It was in the latter part of his life that Moses became the person that pleased God and freed the slaves. He started wrong but ended strong.

II.

David pleased the Lord when he was playing music. Moses pleased the Lord when he was leading a rebellion.

What do you do that pleases God?

It is common to answer this question by appealing to religious duties. You dot every "i" in the religious life and cross every "t" in church, and you please God, right? It is customary for those who run the religious business to interpret the pleasure of God in strictly religious terms.

When I was a kid, the church used an 8-point record system. Each Sunday morning, we checked the boxes on the offering envelope: Attend. Check. On time. Check. Brought Bible. Check. Brought offering. Check. Staying for worship. Check. God is pleased with me. Check.

These 8 things are good. I hope you do them with some regularity. But they mainly functioned to develop organizational strength and to cultivate in a kid or an adult conformity to an organizational norm.

Yes, there are organizational norms in the Christian business. Jesus had 6 points of his own: feed the hungry, give drink to the thirsty, clothe the naked, heal the sick, visit the prisoner, and welcome the stranger. We could call this God's 6-point record system. Paul had his list of expectations. In *Romans,* we read that we should love others, honor each other, work hard, rejoice in hope, be patient in trouble, persist in prayer, help those in need, and practice hospitality (12:6ff). That also is God's 8-point record system.

All those things are good. Doing them pleases God and pleases other people.

Moses brought a ten-point record system down from the mountain. We call it the Ten Commandments. Obey these things, the priests and prophets told the people, and God will be pleased. Then religious leaders added other things: offerings, and festivals, and regulations for the sabbath, plus expectations about farming, harvesting, and giving to the priests. The list of rules and what it meant to please God grew longer and more complicated. The list of those who failed to do those things also grew longer. Religion soon became a game of who is in and who is out, who is pleasing the priests and who is not.

This is the end result of people dedicated to religion. Many of the world's great religions today are full of rules and regulations: what to wear, what to say, where to go and when; how to work and where; what to pray and how often; when to kneel and when to stand; when to speak and when to be silent; what to believe and how to say it; and what to condemn and how to condemn it.

Pleasing God gets complicated. Pleasing God gets distorted. Pleasing God collapses in upon itself.

III.

Paul, the apostle, writes something for us today. He is writing, you remember, from prison, facing an uncertain future. He writes to us as well as to those first Christians in the city of Philippi: "God is working in you, giving you the desire and the power to do what pleases God" (2:12-13).

God is working in you. God is working in you to make you more religious? More obedient? More compliant? More attentive to the religious establishment? I don't think so.

That is precisely where Paul was before he encountered the Risen Jesus. Paul was pursuing all those things before his conversion, prior to his awakening. It was his prequel, we might call it today, to emerging from the cocoon of conformity into the light of new life.

I once had a student call me to talk about the new direction his life had taken. Where did this come from, I asked him. "Remember that book you gave me to read?" and he named the book. "When I read that book, I discovered myself!"[43]

I discovered myself! That is what he said. That is what happened to Paul. That is what conversion is. It is giving up pleasing somebody in the religious world and discovering in yourself a person with whom God is pleased.

That is what God the Almighty said to Jesus, as the man from Galilee began his own journey. "You are my child. I like you. I affirm you. I embrace you. I am happy with you. I am pleased with you. Keep on being yourself, the person I made you to be."

Jesus could have been just another rabbi. Even worse, Jesus could have stayed in his father's carpenter shop, making furniture and fancy trim in the building boom of nearby Sepphoris. But Jesus discovered himself.

---

[43] That student was Lucas Rice. The self-discovery led him to turn from his Baptist upbringing and embrace Orthodox Christianity. I tell his story more fully in *It's About Time: A Memoir of Ministry at Georgetown College* (Bloomington: iUniverse, 2010), p. 37.

Remember Jesus, the emerging teenager in the temple. He wowed the scribes and the rabbis; he worried his parents. But he was discovering himself, his gifts, his calling, and his purpose in life. "I must be about my Father's business," is the way the old King James Version of the Bible translates it (*Luke* 2:49). "I must find my own way to serve God," is the way we might explain it today. "I must know myself and be myself and follow the star as it appears to me, convinced that God is working in me, that God has made me who I am, and that God has filled my soul with ideas and gifts and ambitions and opportunities. I want to be me and thus fulfill the person God has made me to be."

Do you remember the famous scene in the movie *Chariots of Fire*?

Eric Liddell was both a Christian and an athlete; he felt called to be a missionary in China, but he was also a gifted runner. He resisted the pressure to abandon his sport and return to gospel work in China. He felt called to run; he sensed he was born to run. In one particular scene in the movie, he says to his fiancé, "When I run, I feel the pleasure of God."

"When I run, I feel the pleasure of God."

Liddell had been converted from the merely religious to the deeply spiritual. He obeyed the voice that called him to reach down inside of himself, lay hold of that mystery, that voice that calls you to say, "Yes! I can! I must! I will be the person I was born to be."

Liddell represented Great Britain in the 1924 Olympics in Paris. He raced the 100 meters and won the gold medal. He returned to China as a missionary. He died in 1945, in a Japanese internment camp. We remember him today not as a missionary but as a runner. He felt the pleasure of God.

When do you feel the pleasure of God?

When you dig in the good earth?

When you cradle the newborn child?

When you lift your voice and sing to the universe?

When you teach a child the ABCs?

When you introduce a traveler to Victoria Falls or Tel Dan?

When you finish the design of a new product?

When you pray with a neighbor who just lost their father, their job, or their dog?

When do you feel the pleasure of God? Is it when you are doing what you are called to do, not when you are conforming to the religious rules of the day and not when you are pushing down your true self, your deepest aspirations, even your wildest dreams?

You be you, in all the glory and gladness of God; I will be me, in all the craziness of life. Together, we will fulfill all the things the God of the universe has packed into our DNA, into our imaginations, and into the deepest recesses of our souls. That is where God is at work, giving you the desire and giving you the power to be and do what pleases God.

Irenaeus, the great Christian leader of the second century, said it well: "The glory of God is a person, a human, fully alive!"

The glory of God is the human race, fully alive—alive to the glory and the grace that fill the universe, alive to the God who creates, sustains, and redeems all things, alive to the sounds and sights, the touch and the smell of every single thing that God has crafted for the universe.

What pleases God is not one more trip to church, one more dollar in the offering, or one more prayer in unison with others. These are not bad things; they are just not the best things.

The best thing is being the person God made you to be, full of the Spirit, both the human spirit and the Holy Spirit, embracing the world, loving your neighbor, and releasing for the good of the world all that God has put in you.

That is what Moses did, after he got tired of herding sheep on the back side of the mountain. That is what Paul did, after he wearied of tracking down people who were thinking differently, living differently, and singing differently. That is what Jesus did from an early age, by breaking ranks with the norm, by pushing back on family expectations, and by reaching inside of himself to discover himself and his own unique calling.

"You are what you are," John Prine sang in his humorous song "Dear Abby," "and you ain't what you ain't." Discovering this difference is discovering that God is at work in you, giving you the desire to please God and the power to do so.

This openness to being yourself may take you to some crazy places. Just ask the comedian and actor, halfway around the world in Ukraine. His training to stand up and speak and entertain people was, unbeknownst to him and others, preparing him to be just what the world needs at this hour: president of Ukraine, leader of the free world, defender of democracy, and general of the armies of liberty. God is working in President Zelenskyy because he did what he was born to do.

Zelenskyy, like the Wise Men of old, followed the star overhead. You can also. It is never too late. You just might save the nation! You just might compose the perfect chord progression.

Fourteen

Shining Like the Sun

Live clean, innocent lives as children of God,
shining like bright lights in a world full
of crooked and perverse people.
Philippians 2:15

We all like to sing everybody's favorite chorus, "This little light of mine, I'm going to let it shine." It gives voice and sound to the fundamental element of the Christian life, even of human life: that we live in a world with too much darkness, that we live in a world in need of light. To be a Christian is to shine like the sun in a world full of darkness. To be a Christian is to be the light in somebody's darkness. Jesus said (in so many words), "You are the light of the world. Do not put your candle under a bushel" (*Matthew* 5:15).

I.

The Bible describes creation with these words: "In the beginning, God created the heavens and the earth. The earth was formless and empty, and darkness covered the deep waters" (*Genesis* 1:1).

103

Darkness covered the face of everything. That must be the way Ukrainians feel about their country and their civilization. Darkness covers the face of their deep, to use the old phrase. Four million people have fled the country. Entire cities are bombed into ruins. Thousands are dead. It is a darkness of danger, despair, and death. It is the darkness of war. Darkness is a metaphor for the many kinds of evil in the world. Depression, loneliness, and anger are 3 forms of darkness that can overwhelm the individual. Often, there is no one to blame. Often, they are not the result of behavior or attitude. They are part of that original darkness that creeps back into the world.

In that first moment, God said, "Let there be light." And there was light: the greater light to rule the day and the lesser light to rule the night (*Genesis* 1:3, 16). But sometimes the darkness swells up again and overwhelms the light; it sweeps over the soul and pushes the spirit into despair.

Do you know somebody who suffers from depression? It is hard to find any light that can penetrate that darkness, isn't it? Neither laughter nor sunshine can push away that darkness. Some people try one medication after another in their attempt to find a little sunshine.

Poverty, hunger, isolation, and incarceration hide the sun and bring the dark. This is why Jesus told us to give to the poor, feed the hungry, befriend the lonely, and visit the prisoner. Be the light in somebody's darkness. Be a star in somebody's night. Light a candle in somebody's tunnel.

Years ago, I was living in Jerusalem. My mentor, Dale Moody, was there also. He was on sabbatical. I was too young to know what a sabbatical is. We were carted to the Gihon Spring in the Kidron Valley, just on the edge of modern-day Jerusalem. It is a spring of fresh water that naturally flows into the valley, through the Wilderness, and into the Dead Sea. But during the times of the Hebrew prophets and kings, that water was diverted through a tunnel to the other side, the west side, of the Jerusalem ridge. It was redirected to a pool of water that came to be known as the Pool of

Siloam, a place that figures into a story in the gospel accounts of Jesus. "Go to the Pool of Siloam and wash yourself," Jesus told the man, according to the *Gospel of John* (9:11).

That water tunnel is named Hezekiah's Tunnel. It is about 1,800 feet long. It is, in most places, two feet wide. In some places, it is more than 15 feet high, but in other places, it is less than 6 feet high. The water is waist high, which means there is not much room. And, it is dark. "Bring a flashlight with you," the guidebooks say. Many people cannot handle it; it is just too claustrophobic!

Dale Moody and I both had flashlights. But a few yards into the tunnel, his flashlight went dark. When you are in a dark place, you need somebody with a light: a candle, a flashlight, or a cell phone. When you are in a dark place, you need somebody with a light: moonlight, starlight, or sunlight. When you are in a dark place, you need *somebody* who shines like the sun, who shines like a star in a dark sky.

II.

"Live … as children of God, shining like bright lights in a world full of crooked and perverse people" (*Philippians* 2:15).

Paul was in prison when he wrote this letter to the Philippians. For most people, that would be a dark place. Have you ever been in prison? I once spent several hours in jail after being arrested.[44] But a few hours do not count. Many people are in jail for life. Our jails and prisons are bad enough; many jails and prisons around the world are much more dangerous, much more deadly, and much darker.

Yet, Paul was a bright light in that prison. Earlier, he had been in prison in Philippi when an earthquake struck the city, according to the account in chapter 16 of *Acts of the Apostles*. The foundations

---

[44] See Moody, *It's About Time*, p. 48. See also Dwight A. Moody, *On the Other Side of Oddville: Stories on American Religion and Everyday Life* (Macon: Mercer University Press, 2006) p. 158ff.

of the jail were compromised, the jailer was afraid that the prisoners would escape, and he would lose his job (or his head). The account includes this detail: the earthquake struck while Paul and Silas were singing!

There is no indication their music caused the earthquake. But their singing coincided with that memorable shaking. They were singing, and the earth was shaking! Their singing was the sunshine beaming into the darkness of that prison.

Bryan Stevenson is a Harvard-trained lawyer. Instead of taking employment with the federal government or a corporate law firm, Bryan went to work on behalf of people wrongly incarcerated. The jails of the United States are overcrowded, and some of these inmates were wrongly accused, wrongly judged, and wrongly jailed. Brian has spent his life with what he calls the Equal Justice Initiative. He wrote about it in his book, *Just Mercy*. It is inspired by the writing of the Hebrew prophet Micah who challenges us to do justice and love mercy. Watch the movie version of his story, also entitled "Just Mercy."

Bryan Stevenson is a bright light of the Gospel, shining like the sun.

Jeff Bezos is the founder of Amazon. He was once worth an estimated 177 billion dollars. I received in the mail recently two things from Amazon. Their total value is less than $40. That is the difference between him and me! I buy cheap stuff, and he makes billions. Three years ago, Bezos and his wife divorced. Her name is MacKenzie Scott. She is the third wealthiest woman in the world, with a fortune of $62 billion. She has pledged to give away half her fortune. Last year, she gave billions, much of it directed toward HBCUs: Historically Black Colleges and Universities. In 2022, she gave $436 million to Habitat for Humanity.

MacKenzie Scott is a bright light of the Gospel, shining like the sun.

Volodymyr Zelenskyy is the president of Ukraine. I wrote about him in the last chapter. He wasn't always a public leader. For years, he was a comic, an actor, and a performer. Now, he is the president of a nation under attack. He is today a leader of the free world. He is a defender of democracy. He is a hero to his people and to people everywhere.

Volodymyr Zelenskyy is a bright light of the Gospel, shining like the sun.

I do not know if these 3 people are professing Christians. But I do know this: they are living and leading and serving like Jesus himself, who was courageous, confident, compassionate, caring for the least of these, and showing a kindness that can only come from the source of all light and life, the one and only living God.

III.

You and I are not rich, famous, or influential like these three. You and I are simple people, common people, even ordinary people. But we are Christian people. We call Jesus Lord and Savior. We are followers of The Way. We have been baptized into Christ. Paul, in writing to the Romans, said baptism is like being buried with Christ and rising to new life. I remember many details of my baptism, more than 60 years ago. I feel the water. I hear the sounds. I see the people. I remember what the pastor said to me. I was baptized into Christ. I want to live like Christ.

All of us want to be courageous and compassionate and caring people. We want to shine like the stars, shine like the sun, and shine like Jesus, our Lord.

You are shining, Providence. You are shining!

For all of the underfed, malnourished people in our community, you are shining like the sun. Every Sunday for more than a decade, week in and week out, people come to our space here and eat a healthy meal. They are welcomed. They are served. They are fed. Regardless of color or creed, regardless of gender or marital status, regardless of personal history or living situation, they come to Providence; they come to bask in the sun, so to speak. You, Providence, are shining like the sun on all these people.

You are shining like the sun, Providence, upon all the Christian women in our community. They need to hear the gospel word: you are worthy, you are capable, you are called, you are equipped, and you can take the lead and read the word and preach the Gospel; you can take charge and pastor and preach and exercise the servant-leader authority in the Christian community.

For 21 years, it has been so among us. As I wrote above, our founding pastor and her two successors are women. We give thanks for this. We are blinded by the gospel light—it is so close to us! But many of our brothers and sisters in the faith are living in the shadows. They still practice the subordination, even the subjugation of women in the church and in the country. But we have seen the light. And we are shining!

You are shining like the sun, Providence, upon all of our queer brothers and sisters in the county. We receive you as readily and warmly as we receive anyone. We detect no difference between us. We all have the same desire to live and love, to work and rest, to sing and dance, to believe and serve.

During 2022, more than 320 laws targeting LGBTQ people were introduced in state legislatures. This is wickedness, often done in the name of Jesus. We are all human beings, just people, struggling with sin and selfishness and reaching out for grace and mercy.

We are just people, made in the image of God, in need of a little kindness. As John Prine sings in his last song, released a few weeks after his death in 2020, "Sometimes a little tenderness was the best that I could do."[45]

In a world full of hate and meanness and rudeness, a little tenderness goes a long way. In a culture quick to judge and ignore and marginalize, a little kindness feels so good. In a church, the

---

[45] See note 13 above.

Christian church, so full of bad theology and rude vocabulary, a little sweetness is the sunshine we all need.

You are shining like the sun, Providence, and I am thrilled to be living and serving in the sunshine of your love.

Live as children of God, this gospel word says to us today, in the words of the famous apostle. "Live as children of God, shining like stars" in the darkness of the world and the church.

Every time you are gentle to a rude person, you are shining like the sun. Every time you forgive a mean and messy remark, you are shinning like the sun. Every time you open your home and your heart to some displaced or despised person, you are shining like the sun. Every time you speak peace into the whirlwind of provocation and partisanship, you are shining like the sun. Every time you practice self-control in the midst of our indulgent culture, you are shining like the sun. Every time you give generously to a worthy cause or a desperate person, you are shining like the sun. Every time you pause to pray for somebody with cancer or somebody without friends, you are shining like the sun.

You are the light of the world, Jesus said. Light your candle. Hold it high. Let it shine, let it shine, let it shine.

Fifteen

No One Like You

I have no one else like Timothy, who
genuinely cares about your welfare.
Philippians 2:20

Forty-eight years ago, Jan and I had just moved into Judson Hall on the campus of Southern Baptist Seminary in Louisville. One day, we saw another young couple unloading a truck. They were hippies, for sure, straight out of college, with roots in the north. I helped them carry in a sofa. Jan fixed chicken, and we shared a meal. That is the way it all started, our friendship, 48 years ago.

You cannot predict how and where friendships start. High school and college are good bets: teams and clubs and happenstance, for sure. It is purely by accident, often, as it was years ago for Jan and me and our friends, Jude and Marshall Davis.

I think about Marshall when I read this letter Paul wrote. He wrote, "I have no one else like Timothy." Paul was reflecting on friendship, and partnership in the Gospel, and the best of life.

I.

Who are your friends, and how did you meet them?

These are stories that never grow old. Perhaps your post-sermon card needs to be a note to a friend, one close at hand or one far away. Perhaps it needs to be an offer of friendship. "Let's be friends."

Paul writes here about two other friends, but we know that he had many. His letters are filled with references to people. We often focus too much on the doctrines, the controversies, the ethical dilemmas, or the religious movement that came to be called Christianity. We give too little time to the people. In the truest of true things, it is the people who matter. In the document we call *Romans,* Paul wrote about Aquilla and Pricilla, the itinerant and transplanted business couple that set Apollos straight about Jesus and the Spirit. "They once risked their lives for me," (16:3-4). I once pastored a church in Pittsburgh that was full of transplanted people, folk who had the spirit and talent of Pricilla and Aquilla. I grew to love ministry to people on the road, away from home.

Paul wrote about Junia, whom he called an apostle, and about Phoebe, who delivered the famous letter to the church at Rome: "They ... became followers of Christ before I did," he wrote (*Romans* 16:7).

In this letter to Philippi, Paul named Epaphroditus (2:25), who brought to the imprisoned Paul the supplies of food and money from the Philippians. He named two women, Euodia and Syntyche (4:2), and urged them to patch up their differences. But chief on the list of those friends named by Paul is the much younger Timothy.

Paul and Timothy were at least a generation apart. The famous apostle was a mentor to the young man, and a supervisor, we might say, in his Gospel work. "I hope to send Timothy to you soon," he wrote in this letter (2:19). "He has proved himself," is the way the old man in jail talked about the young man on the move (2:22).

But they were also friends. "I have no one else like Timothy," Paul wrote.

I have had many friends a generation older than I am: men and women who taught me, formed me, loved me, and forgave me. I have many young friends: youth I dipped into the baptismal waters, students who came through my classes, and young preachers who helped make the Academy of Preachers such a marvelous ministry for a decade.

Who are your friends?

II.

Friendship is a wonderful thing. A former member of this church wrote this week on social media: "Of all the interactions I had during my 15 plus years in Hendersonville, I made the most lasting friends at Providence."

She was responding to an article I had posted on my Facebook page. It was sent to me by our member and gospel minister, James Garrison, and is titled "The Lonely Crowd: Churches Dying Due to Friendlessness."[46] Thank you, James. That was the action of a friend.

"They're nice to you, but no one becomes your friend," is the way the author (Mike Frost) summed up the situation at many churches. He concluded his appeal with these words: "Before hosting any more conferences or seminars on vision-casting, living your best life, or finding your spiritual gift, how about we start equipping people in friendship-making?"

Frost then gave these statistics, comparing 1985 to 2004. Researchers asked the question, "Over the last 6 months, who are the people with whom you discussed matters of importance to you?" In 1985, 59% of respondents listed 3 or more people. In 2004, only 37% responded 3 or more. Twenty-five percent of the 2004 respondents said, zero!

---

[46] The article is by Mike Frost and is found on the website of Churchleaders.com, posted on January 8, 2022.

There is a lot of attention given to music in worship, and preaching, and buildings, and programs, and doctrine, and in these days, politics. But perhaps the biggest issue in church life, or the biggest issue in everyone's life is friendship or the lack thereof!

Jesus said, "I no longer call you slaves.... Now you are my friends" (*Gospel of John* 15:15). We could update that language to say, "We no longer call you members, or guests, or prospects, or ministers; we call you friends."

Here at Providence, we are using this wonderful two-tier theme: *Sing for joy and live with hope.* My son and I put lettering on the back wall, the words taken from the King James Versions of the Hebrew prophet Micah, "Do justice, love mercy, and walk humbly with God" (6:8). These two summaries of gospel living are terrific. But perhaps we need something like "Make Friends. Be Friends."

Mr. Rogers, a life-long native of Pittsburgh, shaped a generation of children by asking, "Will you be my friend?" The book that tells his story is simply titled *You Are My Friend.*[47]

Maybe the natural and supernatural order of things is, "Be my friend," before we ask questions like "Do you want to come to church?" or "Are you ready to be baptized?" or "Are you a member?" Or even, "Are you a Christian?"

There is a lot of mystery and happenstance in friendship. My best buddy in grade school was a boy named Homer Reaves. He sat behind me and was the object of my overactive mouth. I still hold the school record for writing the most times, "I will not talk."[48] I moved away from Lexington after the fourth grade and missed him very much. Sometime later, when my family went to visit my grandmother in Lexington, I called him. This is how it went. "Hello, this is Dwight." He responded, "This is Homer." There was a long

---

[47] Amiee Reid, *You Are My Friend: The Story of Mister Rogers and His Neighborhood* (New York: Abrams Press, 2018).
[48] Kenwick Elementary School, later renamed for the principal Julia Ewing, and still later, de-commissioned and sold, Lexington, Kentucky.

pause, a very long pause. I did not know what to say, until finally I said, "I'd better go. Bye." And he hung up the phone.

It was awkward then, but it is funny now! Years later, we met serendipitously at the CBF annual meeting. He was a member of a Baptist church in New Jersey. We had a good time remembering things together. Not all friendships outlast all the things that break them up, including separation and distance. But there *is* a friend who will be your friend forever.

III.

In a few moments, we will sing the grand old gospel song, "What a Friend We Have in Jesus." I love the song, and I hope you do as well. For some, it might not measure up to the contemporary praise chorus or the sophisticated anthem. But it calls us to sing about what is at the center of the spiritual life: friendship, especially friendship with Jesus.

Jesus was a friend. We have scant record of Jesus going to a worship service, let alone a Sunday School class or a discipleship retreat. He went fishing with his friends, went to their homes to eat, walked a lot of places with them, and shared what they had. They talked about Holy Scripture. They listened, as random people brought their questions and confusions. As far as we know, there was no book club, no softball team, no youth choir, and no two-week revival—just a lot of hanging out and walking and talking.

But there was something! It was something that bound them together as people, as believers, as children of God, as travelers on a journey, and as citizens of heaven.

Together, they fed the crowds and comforted the sick. Together, they witnessed the glory of God and struggled with their own weaknesses. Together, they gathered the children and scattered the skeptics. Together, they prayed and slept and prepared for the worse. It is not so much that they looked each other in the eyes and confessed their love; that is the ritual for lovers, for erotic love, as C.S. Lewis explained in his famous book, *The Four Loves.*[49] No, these people, men and women, stood side by side and looked at the world, at the crowds, at the Bible, at the city, and at the cross.

This is the week we think about Jesus as a friend. He and his friends walked through Jericho and went to the house of Zacchaeus. He and his friends stopped at the home of their friends in Bethany— Mary, Martha, and Lazarus. He and his friends went, for the last time, to Temple Mount. There, Jesus confounded the authorities and confronted the critics. Jesus and his friends ate together for the last time and prayed together before the big day. Jesus and his friends faced the trauma of rejection, violence, and separation.

Not all of Jesus' friends were loyal to the end. But Jesus was and still is a faithful friend. Jesus was a friend of sinners then and now, a friend of those weak and fearful, and a friend to us when we are full of doubt, anger, and anxiety. Jesus is your friend today. Jesus sees you and knows you and hears you. Jesus stays with you today and tomorrow. Jesus knows your name and is always glad you came!

What a friend you have in Jesus!

God only knows who else in this sanctuary or on this broadcast might be your friend today. Reach out to some friend. Say thanks, or say, "Be my friend today." Call a friend today and thank them, bless them, and offer them another dose of your own love and loyalty. Call out to Jesus, the living Lord, the unseen friend, and say, "I need you today, Jesus. Come, walk with me."

My friend Marshall sent me an article this week. It is titled "The remarkable moment John Prine first met Bob Dylan in New York City."[50] Even though I have not seen Marshall in several years—he lives in New Hampshire, and I live in a different state every year, it

[49] C. S. Lewis, *The Four Loves* (London: Geoffrey Bles, 1960). See especially the chapter on friendship.
[50] The article was written by Tom Taylor and posted on faroutmagazine.co.uk on April 7, 2022.

seems—he remembered me and knew my need, my interests, and my joys. That's a real friend, don't you think?

Jesus is sending you a message today. I am the messenger. Here is the message: Jesus is your friend. Jesus is near to you today. Jesus knows your every need, every dream, every struggle, every hope, and every disappointment. Jesus is ready to listen, to talk, and to travel with you. Let Jesus be your friend today.

Today, take this moment and be a friend with somebody, with Jesus. There is no one like Jesus.

Sixteen

I Never Get Tired

I never get tired of telling you these things,
and I do it to safeguard your faith.
Philippians 3:1

The words made famous by Paul Robeson tell one story: "I gets weary and sick of trying, I'm tired of livin' but I'm scared of dyin' ...." It is the lament of the laboring man and woman, working long, hard hours under the whip of the white man.[51] Such is the sad refrain of so many around the world, even today: people who have no choice of their labor or of the conditions of their work. Many, even in these United States, are weary of work and tired of living.

How different is the situation with the great apostle Paul! He writes from his jail cell, "I never get tired." He is talking about his coaching those new disciples in Philippi. Over and over again, he tells them to trust God, to give thanks, to follow Jesus, to forgive others, and, especially, to rejoice! "I never get tired of telling you to rejoice." Later in this short letter, he writes, "I say it again—rejoice!" (4:4)

---

[51] From the song "Ol' Man River" from the 1927 Broadway musical *Showboat* by Oscar Hammerstein II based on a 1926 novel by Edna Ferber by the same name. Paul Robeson (1898-1976) played the part of Joe in the 1936 film version of the show, singing this famous song.

Sometimes we say to employees, to children, to athletes or musicians, "If I have to tell you one more time …." That is a sign of exasperation, of getting tired of teaching and coaching. I've felt like that many times. But Paul begins this section of his wonderful letter with a striking assertion, "I never get tired."

I.

This statement is the beginning of a string of short, sharp declarations of what is important to Paul. I call them "I-Statements." Let me quote them, as they are translated in the *New Living Translation.*

"I never get tired" (3:1).
"I consider them worthless" (3:7).
"I want to know Christ" (3:10).
"I press on" (3:12, 14).
"I love you" (4:1).
"I praise the Lord" (4:10).
"I can do everything" (4:13).
"I have all I need" (4:18).

These 8 statements, taken together, constitute what we might today call a testimony. If we fill out the sentences a bit and read them together, we will hear Paul, the great lion of God, describe his attitude toward life, faith, and God.

I never get tired of talking about Jesus. I consider my prior religious stuff nothing but trash. I want to know Jesus Christ and live in the power of his resurrection. Because of that, I press on to be what God has called me to be. I love you, my brothers and sisters in the Lord. I praise the Lord for our partnership in gospel work. Because God strengthens me, I can do all things God desires. And for now, I have all I need.

Isn't that a terrific testimony? It is short. It is positive. It is centered on Jesus, the risen Lord. It affirms others. It pulls us into the richness and the beauty of Paul's spiritual life.

What makes this even more special are the circumstances in which Paul was living, writing, and testifying at the time. He had been arrested, again, and thrown into prison. He was dependent on friends to provide his food, bring him news, take dictation for his letters, and keep him company. Paul had no permanent home, and he does not appear to have been married. He never mentions blood brothers or sisters, a mother or a father, or even aunts, uncles, or cousins.[52]

Nevertheless, Paul had a great testimony.

What kind of testimony do *you* have? Can you repeat these words of Paul as your own? Do they describe your spirit, your attitude, and your disposition? Do they describe the person you want to be?

Or, is your attitude more like this: "I am tired of having to do so much of the work. So much of what I have been doing is really worthless. I know Jesus Christ, I guess, but I don't feel any of the resurrection power. I am trying to be what God wants, but I am tired of some of the Christians I have to work with and listen to. I'm not so sure about this partnership we call 'church.' I try to be a spiritual person, but I don't think I measure up. I look around our congregation and think of all we need: more people, more volunteers, more money, and more time."

II.

A first step toward a richer, deeper spiritual life is to start where Paul started. Let him be our guide, our coach. He writes, "I never get tired ... ." Paul is describing his attitude toward teaching the way of Christ, of calling them to joy, of leading those first believers in

---

[52] But see *Acts of the Apostles* 23:16, where a sister and a nephew are mentioned.

Philippi to celebrate what they have, rather than bemoaning what they do not have.

The one thing we all can have is joy. Paul calls us to do what we enjoy and to keep doing things that bring us joy. He says it like this: Rejoice! But translating it like that makes it sound too religious, too churchy, and too spiritual. Paul is not telling us to be in a better mood, or to raise our hands and shout to God, or to perform some expected religious ritual. He is not looking at disheartened or disgruntled people and saying, "You better get joyful, or else."

No, he is testifying, "I never get tired of coaching you in your walk with Jesus. That brings me a lot of joy."

So, I ask you the question: what brings you joy? What habit, or pastime, or task makes you happy? About what can you say, "I never get tired of doing that!"? This is the key to the spiritual life: embracing those things that bring you joy.

I made a list of things that make me happy, things that never tire me out. I never get tired of listening to music, especially if it is Tchaikovsky, or a church choir, or John Prine! I never get tired of preaching the Gospel of Jesus Christ. I never get tired of watching *Seinfeld*, even when I know exactly what is about to be said. I never get tired of reading, especially history, or historical fiction, or even the news. I never get tired of eating ice cream. I never get tired of being out in the sunshine, whether working in the yard, or walking on the beach, or just sitting on the porch and feeling the warmth of the sun. I never get tired of having lunch with a friend. I never get tired of writing a letter, a sermon, a commentary, or a book. I never get tired of being recognized for something good I have done, in public or in private, with a card, a letter, or a phone call. I never get tired of being on the road again to visit some new or familiar place. Keeping these things in my life makes me a happier person, makes me a joyful person, and makes me a better companion.

What about you? Find a card and make your list. Talk about this over lunch today. Tell your spouse, your children, or your mom what makes you happy.

Is it playing baseball or working a puzzle? Perhaps it is planting a garden or swimming laps? Maybe it is hosting a luncheon or watching a movie. For some of you, it is reading poetry or caring for grandkids.

What makes you happy? About what can you say, "I never get tired of"?

Paul found his sweet spot. He spent a long time looking for it. In the next chapter, I pick up his statement, "I now consider it all trash." But here, my message for you is this: find the things about which you can say, "I never get tired," and work them into your life.

III.

Many of us spend a long time looking for the source of true joy. Paul found it in coaching others in their walk with the Lord. Your sweet spot of living may not be religious, but it will certainly be spiritual because it will nourish your spirit. In that sense, all of us need to be less religious and more spiritual.

Some of you may need to pull back from your religious duties, in order to be a more spiritual person. Some of you may need to embrace a religious practice, in order to find the center of your spiritual life. Each of us has our own path, and sometimes those paths cross in a group, a team, a choir, or a congregation.

You may say, "Teaching children about the life of Jesus brings me great joy." You may say, "Singing in the gospel choir brings me great joy." You may say, "Serving hungry people a hot meal around a table brings me great joy." You may say, "Giving my money so that a talented student can go on a mission trip brings me great joy." You may say, "Opening my home for a Bible study with my friends brings me great joy." You may say, "Hiking through these beautiful mountains brings me great joy."

In 2013, my dad died, 65 years after finding his source of joy in life. He graduated from the university with a degree in mathematics and started a career teaching in high school. But somewhere along the way, he changed courses and took a new direction. He embraced what today we call the ministry, or what I like to call gospel work. George Thomas Moody died at the age of 90. He and I were very close friends. I admired him greatly, and he continues to inspire me. I preached his funeral sermon and wrote the obituary that appeared in the paper. This is the way I concluded that public description of him: "The family requests that generous memorial gifts be given to one of these 3 funds: the Church in Murray, the Seminary in Kentucky, or a Christian fellowship in California. More than that, we urge all who knew him to honor his life by practicing kindness to everyone, telling someone about Jesus and his love, and organizing people for a good and godly purpose."

I want to emphasize that last one: "organizing people for a good and godly purpose." These 3 gospel practices brought much joy to my dad. He would say today, if he were called upon to give a testimony, "I never get tired of being kind to strangers, of telling people about Jesus, and of organizing people for a good and godly purpose." We still need those gifts today.

Find what it is that brings joy to your soul, and God will give you the gift of never getting tired of it.

Seventeen

I Consider It Trash

I have discarded everything else, counting it all as garbage,
so that I could gain Christ and become one with him.
Philippians 3:9

The United Nations now estimates that 8 million people will flee Ukraine as refugees. Some will go back, but others will scatter around the world, putting behind them their old life in Ukraine. Property, business, family, friends, plans, and more will be discarded on their way to a future.

All of us have had to put behind us some things: a toxic relationship, an old job, a failing marriage, outworn ideas, even convictions or beliefs. We have, as it were, dumped them into one of the green totes, rolled it to the street, and left it for the trashman to pick up.

That is what happened to this itinerant organizer and evangelist two thousand years ago. "I once thought these things were valuable," Paul writes in this little letter. "But now, I consider them worthless .... I have discarded everything..." (*Philippians* 3:7).

I consider it trash, he writes, worthless, garbage.

These words, spoken from Paul's heart, speak to us today a good gospel word. It is time to put some things behind us and embrace what God has put before us.

I.

This statement, "I consider it trash," is the second of 8 simple sentences that together comprise the Christian testimony of Paul, the Apostle. A testimony is a statement describing our relationship with Jesus, our faith in God, and our experience of these religious and spiritual realities. I hope you have a testimony. I hope you can write in a paragraph or a page something that expresses how you feel, what you think, and why you take the name of Jesus Christ.

Paul embedded these 8 statements in this letter. In the previous chapter, I stitched these statements together into one paragraph:

> I never get tired of talking about Jesus. I consider all my prior religious stuff nothing but trash. I want to know Jesus Christ and live in the power of his resurrection. Because of that, I press on to be what God has called me to be. I love you, my brothers and sisters in the Lord. I praise the Lord for our partnership in gospel work. Because God strengthens me, I can do all things God desires. And for now, I have all I need.

In this chapter, I want to focus on one piece of the testimony: "I consider it trash." I consider it—all my prior religious stuff— nothing but trash.

Are there things you need to push out of your life? Are there some elements of your religion that need to be discarded? Do you have things you once treasured that need to be dumped?

Maybe a few moments of reading this two-thousand-year-old testimony of Paul will give you reason to dump some stuff, motivation to leave some things at the curb, and determination to cleanse your own soul and move into a future you long to embrace.

II.

Paul lists the things he is dumping: "I was circumcised … . I am a pure-blooded Jew … . I was a Pharisee … . I persecuted the church … . I obeyed the Law without fault" (3:5-6).

That is a impressive list of religious accomplishments. Can I translate it into our religious culture?

> I was baptized at the age of nine. I was raised in a thoroughly Christian family. Even my grandparents were devout Christians. I was the champion of the Bible Drill as a child and honored as a Bible teacher as an adult. I denounced false Christians, like the liberals who deny the Bible or the fundamentalists who worship the Bible. I have walked the straight and narrow path marked by Jesus and his disciples. I have obeyed all the rules of our church.

What was it about these things that turned them into trash? What is wrong with baptism? Shouldn't I rejoice in my Christian upbringing? Isn't teaching the Bible a good thing? Should not we all desire to live a disciplined and devout life?

These are the same questions that could have been put to Paul, that could have stymied his search for authentic faith, and that could have prevented him from the conversion that has shaped the Western world.

Many of these trashy things were valuable. There was something good about initiation into the faith and practice of Judaism. Paul was introduced to the Hebrew Bible, the Old Testament as we call it, the Torah as they knew it. He learned about creation and exodus, he sang the songs of the psalms, he recited the words of the law, and he felt the impact of the prophets who said, "Let justice roll down like waters and righteousness like an ever-flowing stream" (*Amos* 5:14, KJV). Surely, this was all good.

Sometimes, even good things need to be left behind, abandoned, or trashed. When the U. S. Army left Afghanistan, they left behind 8 billion dollars of good, useable equipment!

What was it that motivated Paul to turn his eyes from these things? What was missing in his religion that he found on the road to Damascus? Why was he so quick and ready to lay aside these good things and go in a new direction?

Paul had a powerful encounter with Jesus, the Risen Lord. While traveling to Damascus to continue his assault on those who deviated from the narrow way of Judaism, he saw a light and heard a voice and fell to the ground.[53] Something new, and fresh, and compelling was presented to him. It was a new way to live, a new vision of what it meant to be human, a new understanding of God. No wonder Paul wrote in another place, "Anyone who belongs to Christ has become a new person. The old life is gone; a new life has begun!" (*Second Corinthians* 5:17).

I once sat across the table from a young man. "Are you from North Carolina?" I asked.

"No," he said, "I'm from Montana."

"How did you get here?" I asked, just to make conversation.

He surprised me with his answer: "A minister from here drove out to Montana and rescued me from my abusive, narcissistic, and violent father. I've been here for 8 years."

I did not know what to say.

Here was a young man who could say with Paul, "I consider it trash, everything I had; it is all worthless. I am moving on to something true, and rich, and beautiful. I am ready to *sing for joy and live with hope*."

---

[53] The story is told in *Acts of the Apostles*, chapter 9.

Many people have put ugliness behind them to embrace the beauty of life, have said goodbye to violence to say hello to peace and tranquility, have abandoned the road that leads only to promiscuity, pornography, and sensual pleasure to take the road that leads to delight and contentment and joy.

In hundreds of buildings, sanctuaries, and storefronts, men and women are desperate to leave behind addictions to alcohol, drugs, and a culture of self-destruction and to enter a life of what Paul described in his letter to the Galatians as "love, joy, peace, steadfastness, kindness, goodness, faithfulness, gentleness, and self-control" (*Galatians* 5:22).

Remember the Penses children? Susan, Lucy, Peter, and Edmond left the rambling two story house of the professor, walked through the wardrobe, and entered Narnia. They left behind some things, good and bad, to enter into things that were so much better.[54]

This is the testimony of many people: I consider it trash. I'm going to toss aside some things I've been thinking, some things I've been doing, and some things I've been keeping in order. I want to go in a new direction, with new energy, and with new ambition.

This is what the Bible means by "new life in Christ." This is what Jesus means by his phrase "born again." This is what the Gospel means by conversion. This is what we see in baptism: we go all the way under to signify the death and burial of some things, and we come all the way up, dripping wet to signify the beginning of a new life.

I'm putting out the trash, Paul writes here, to make way for the newness that Jesus Christ is bringing to my house, my soul, and my life.

---

[54] Their story is told in *The Narnia Chronicles* by C. S. Lewis.

III.

It is not just people like us who need this sort of trash day. It is nations, churches, and families. As a nation, we looked around at the despicable way we treated black people in our nation; we looked and said, "These trashy policies, and attitudes, and behaviors need to go." There are many other policies and practices that we need to consider trash and haul to the curb. We need to move on to a better future. We need to dream of a better day, a day without prejudice, without violence, and without addictions. Like Rev. Dr. Martin Luther King, Jr., we all need a dream!

What about our congregation? Do we need a new day, a new plan, and a new spirit? Do we need to take to the curb the old ideas of what it means to succeed, of what it means to worship, and of what it means to serve? Do we need to embrace new ideas, new opportunities and new realities of being disciples of Christ in our place and time?

I recently spent a long time on the phone with a friend who lives in Tulsa, Oklahoma.[55] I was driving over the mountains to Kentucky. Every three minutes, my phone lost contact, and he had to call back: again, again, and again. He was talking about post-pandemic gospel work and how their congregation was emerging from the dark night of the soul that we called COVID.

"People have left and are never coming back," he said. I said, "Amen."

"Programs have dissolved and will never take form again," he explained. I said, "That's for sure."

"Church life is different now than it was before," he concluded. I said, "Tell me about it!"

We were having church in two states, across the mountains and the wide Mississippi!

---

[55] Rev. Dr. David Emery, pastor of Harvard Avenue Christian Church of Tulsa.

The Lord spoke to me that day on the road to Knoxville through the voice of my friend in Tulsa. As he explained the three-pronged advance of their church, I thought about the three things our Providence Church needs to emphasize: the Sunday worship here and everywhere (through the broadcast); the Lord's Day meal we serve next door to those who need soup and sandwiches more than they need a song and sermon; and the everyday outreach of gospel teaching and testifying, of listening and learning, of connecting with those who have no interest in walking into this sanctuary or joining an organization called "church."

We need to put aside our fears and our failures, our hesitations and our inhibitions, our practices and our preferences, and go where we have not gone before.

On a recent Palm Sunday, a dozen or more of us picked up balloons and palm branches and started walking. Some of you were skeptical, and most of us were unsure. What are we doing, and why, and what will come of this?

We started in the back lot and walked up Schepper Street and turned left onto Oakland Street. We waved our branches and started singing, "This little light of mine, I'm going to let it shine." We took the short cut down Killarney Street over to Patton Street and turned left. We held our helium-filled balloons, even as our souls were filled with hesitation.

The sky was blue, and sun was bright, and hardly anybody saw what we were doing. No doors opened, no curtains parted, and no lights switched on. But something was happening—not to them, the people who live around our church campus and don't even know we are here, but to us, the hearty souls walking, singing, and giving glory to God.

We walked down Highland Avenue, past the old hospital on the left and the Confederate flag on the right. We were feeling better, and I have it all on video! We turned left onto Regal Street, singing, "Hide it under a bushel, no, I'm going to let it shine."

I was telling this story to an old friend in Lexington on Wednesday night, and she asked, "What did you do on this walk?" I said, we sang, and celebrated Jesus, the Risen Lord. But what I thought to myself was this: "We put ourselves in a place where God could do something in us, among us, and through us.

It was not the community God reached that day; it was us. As we walked back into the church, we said to one another, "That was alright. That wasn't so bad. That was good. I'm glad we did that. Let's do it again next year."

But I say to you today, let's not wait until next year. Let's get out of this sanctuary and off of our property, out of our comfort zone and into our mission zone. Let's take to the curb the idea that people need to come to us and sit in our pews and sing our songs. Let's repackage our Gospel and hand deliver it to anybody and everybody, wherever they might be.

A dozen or so of us marched around the block. Are a dozen people enough? Are 12 apostles enough? There are 16 of us here today. Is that enough? We are the micro-church. We are the future of the faith. We are nimble enough to change our ways and courageous enough to consider some things trash. I helped my sister clean out her garage this week. She picked up piece after piece and said, "I'm getting rid of this. This goes in the trash." We must do the same.

I am going to make the first move in this march toward tomorrow. Vote me in as your pastor! Last year, I began as your Sunday Preacher. In December, I agreed to the title Interim Pastor, for a period of 6 months. But now, it is time: just elect me as you pastor!

In the *Acts of the Apostles*, the writer describes the unusual things that happened to the people on the day of Pentecost: the sound of a rushing wind, the flame of fire settling on each one, the testimonies one after the other of people who were living for Jesus, the charge of drunkenness from a stranger, the explanation and sermon of Simon Peter, and the invitation to all the people to get up and do something.

It concludes with these sentences: "Those who believed what Peter said were baptized and added to the church that day—about 3,000 in all. All the believers devoted themselves to the apostles' teaching, and to fellowship, and to sharing in meals … and to prayer" (*Acts of the Apostles* 2:42-47).

This Pentecostal experience and these Pentecostal practices (learning, hosting, sharing, and praying) still call us to a journey with the Lord Jesus Christ. Are you ready?[56]

---

[56] In the sermon upon which this chapter is based, I announced I would "join the church" on Pentecost Sunday, 2022, and invited others to also join the church on that day. As it turned out, no other person opted to "go with me" that Sunday. But I know now that "joining the church" is part of an old way of doing church, one dominated by organizational concerns, like membership and policies. The mission is not to get people out there to come into our space, sing our songs, pray our prayers, and listen to our sermons. It is to mobilize our people and our resources to empower people "out there" to become the people they are meant to be and to do the work they are meant to do. What is important is what goes on in their homes, their worksites, and in their minds and hearts.

Eighteen

I Want to Know Christ

*I want to know Christ and experience the mighty
power that raised him from the dead.*
Philippians 3:10

I like people with ambition.

For twenty years, I worked with young adults: first at the college and then with the Academy of Preachers. I met and talked with hundreds of students. I often asked them this question: What is your ambition? I have been stunned at how many of them had no answer, had never thought about it, and had nothing to say.

What is *your* ambition? Do you want to own your own company, write a book, read a book, raise a family, travel to Paris, or London, or Jerusalem? What is your ambition?

Sometimes, we tag ambitious people as ruthless, or selfish, or willing to run over others to reach some personal goal. For years, I have said to those around me, especially those I supervised or led, "My ambition is to help you get where you want to go." That is the way I feel as a pastor. I want to help you, the congregation, get where you want to go or become what you want to become. I also feel that way about you as individuals: Do you have ambitions for life, for work, for health, for faith?

What is your ambition as a believer? How would you state your deepest desire about spiritual things: I want to forgive some people who wronged me; or, I want to understand the Bible; or, I want to have more confidence to talk to people about Jesus; or, I want to have a spiritual ministry to people; or, I want to work through my doubts and embrace great faith; or I want to know my purpose in life?

What is your ambition in the things of Christ?

Paul has a good word to us when he writes, "I want to know Christ." It is a simple, straightforward expression of his ambition. "I want to experience the power of Jesus' resurrection. I want to share in the sufferings of Jesus. I want to attain, at the end of the age, a place in the resurrection of the righteous."

These three ancillary statements flow out of his fundamental desire, his ambition, to know Christ.

I.

Paul did not always have these three ambitions. When we piece together his life—beginning when he was known as Saul—we can surmise that he began with an ambition to be a scholar. He left Tarsus in Asia Minor and came to Jerusalem to study Torah, the Hebrew Bible. He became a student of the leading Torah scholar of his day, Gamaliel. Saul was exceedingly bright, disciplined, and ambitious.

These, I can tell you, are wonderful traits in a student. Too many students at all levels of learning are dull, careless, and indifferent. God, give us more students who are bright, disciplined, and ambitious!

Saul had ambitions to be at the top of his Torah class, a scholar of note, and a person of intellectual power. These are good things. But this ambition did not satisfy Saul.

As we read between the lines of the gospel material, we learn that Saul was overtaken by another ambition: to protect Judaism from distortion, from error, and from change. Like many conservatives in all arenas of life, he feared the threat of new ideas, new leaders, and new movements. New things challenge the old order; new ideas threaten the old orthodoxy, and new ways of thinking and doing undermine the old ways of thinking and doing. This is particularly true in the realm of religion.

Saul took up the defense of the old ways. He watched the Jesus movement take root and spread. He listened to their ideas, their stories, and their parables, and was alarmed. "This will upend everything," he surmised.

We have no evidence that Saul ever met Jesus, that he ever saw Jesus, or that he ever heard Jesus teach or preach or question the authorities. Saul did not know Jesus, the rabbi of Nazareth, Jesus, the miracle worker, or Jesus, the populist preacher of the rule of God, the community of faith, and the good news of shalom. Saul did not know Jesus, the son of Mary, the brother of James, and the friend of sinners, far and wide. Saul did not know Jesus, full of the Spirit and speaking a fresh word from the Lord.

But the Jesus he heard about frightened him. Saul was fearful of the message of Jesus. Saul was fearful of the success of Jesus. Saul was fearful of the movement that emerged after the death of Jesus.

Saul embraced a new ambition: defend the faith of his fathers. Saul took on a new task: suppress this populist movement that had spread from Jerusalem to Samaria, to Syria, to Damascus, to Antioch, and perhaps even to Rome itself. Saul threw all of his considerable talents and energies into this new calling: stopping the gospel movement known simply as The Way (*Acts of the Apostles* 9:2 and elsewhere).

"Send me to Damascus," Saul told the Jerusalem authorities. "I will put a stop to this Jesus nonsense, this pseudo-Jewish religion, this distortion of our faith. Give me the power, and I will force these deviants to renounce their ideas and abandon their ways."

Yes, Saul had a new ambition.

It is not a bad thing to change. It is not a weakness of the self to start in one direction, animated by one vision of life, then to change directions, to respond to new influences, new opportunities, and new joys. When we are young, we think one thing; but often as we grow, we think another thing. We change our minds. We change our loyalties. We change our values. We change jobs, careers, even vocations. This is a good thing.

But for Saul, change was not a good thing. It took him from good to bad. To his intense religious nature, he added the worst of all dispositions: violence. We first hear of Saul in this report from *Acts of the Apostles*: "The Jewish leaders were infuriated by Stephen's accusation against them, and they shook their fists at Stephen in rage. But Stephen, full of the Holy Spirit, gazed steadily into heaven and saw the glory of God. He saw Jesus standing in the place of honor, and he said, 'Look! I see the heavens opened and the Son of Man standing in the place of honor at God's right hand.'[57] Then the religious leaders rushed at Stephen and dragged him out of the city and began to stone him. His accusers took off their coats and laid them at the feet of a young man named Saul" (7:54ff).

They took their coats and laid them at the feet of a young man named Saul.

Here is the genesis of his change of attitude. Here is the beginning of his new ambition. Here is the launch of his new purpose in life. He put aside his spiritual and intellectual gifts and took up the sword and spirit as the defender of the faith.

He had a new ambition!

---

[57] I realize there is a tension in how see and understand the place and work of Jesus after his resurrection. Here, quoting from the *Acts of the Apostles*, Jesus is seen seated in a place of honor, perhaps on a throne, whereas in chapter 12, I describe Jesus as still at work in the world, responding to the needs of people. But a royal position of honor and power need not be taken as without responsibility or activity. In fact, it may be understood as an intensification of authority and energy, which, in Jesus' case, would mean a broader, deeper commitment to caring for the people of his kingdom.

When it comes to ambition, I've had a conversion or two. I grew up like all boys in Kentucky with dreams of playing for Adolph Rupp or playing in Rupp Arena. My son, Allan, actually lived that dream, playing in a Kentucky state basketball championship tournament in Rupp Arena.

I had to give up my hoop dreams and settle for preaching. In those days, we all wanted to be like Billy Graham. My earliest speeches in high school tournaments were all about the style and substance of Mr. Graham.

Then, I met Dale Moody. For almost 50 years, he was the preeminent theologian among Baptists in the South. He came to our college to speak, and I was mesmerized. He was on sabbatical in Jerusalem when I lived there, and he said to me, "I'm saving you a seat in my theology class." For the next decade or two, I aspired to be like Dale Moody: biblical, evangelical, and ecumenical, learned in every way and in command of every lectern and pulpit.

But I am neither Billy Graham nor Dale Moody.

It takes time to find yourself, to embrace your own gifts and callings, and to be content with who you are, where you are going, and what you can do. This is a great journey: for me, for you, for Saul the scholar, and for Saul the soldier of God.

Saul discovered himself one day on the road to Damascus. Yes, I know, we often describe this event as his discovery of Jesus. But it was more than that. On that journey and in the days that followed, Saul did discover Jesus, but Saul also discovered his own purpose in life. Saul discovered himself.

He was on his way to investigate rumors of a renegade group of Jews, reading Torah, talking Jesus, who were perhaps even hobnobbing with Gentiles. On the road, he was blinded by a light and surprised by a voice. "Who are you?" Saul asked. "I am Jesus!" came the answer (as the story is narrated in *Acts of the Apostles*, chapter 9).

It was a stunning turn of events. That episode was the road sign for a new direction in his journey, a new purpose for his considerable powers, a new ambition for his consequential life.

From that day, Paul dates his calling to preach the Gospel to the Gentiles. From that day, Paul embraces his new ambition, to know Christ, his resurrection power, and his redemptive suffering. Years later, when others opposing this new mission threw him into jail somewhere in the Mediterranean world, Paul wrote this little letter to his friends in Philippi and also to us. He summed up his convictions, his purpose, and his ambition in life: "I want to know Christ."

III.

I would like to meet Jesus, wouldn't you?

Sometimes I fantasize about hosting a dinner party of people I really want to meet: historical figures, like Marco Polo, Joan of Arc, and Abraham Lincoln; influential thinkers like Socrates, and Augustine, and Einstein; biblical personalities like Abraham, Esther, Isaiah; or celebrities like Mark Twain, Martin Luther King, Jr., and John Prine. I'd like to be able to say, "Oh, yes, I know Dolly Parton. I know Michael Jordan. I know Jimmy Carter."

Yes, I'd like to have a one-on-one with Jesus. I have a lot of Nicodemus in me. I have a lot of questions. I am full of curiosity. "What do you mean, Jesus, when you talk about 'born again'? What is this kingdom of God you keep referring to? Are you aware that people want to kill you?"

Yes, I want to know Jesus in this way. Is his hair long like mine? Does he wear it in a ponytail? Will Jesus listen to my questions? Are his teeth straight, his beard trimmed, his hands groomed? Can Jesus tell a joke? Can he take a joke? Does he like BarBQ? Ice cream? Is he a vegan?

That would be wonderful, don't you think?

Maybe someday!

But today, I want to know Christ: his spirit, his attitude, and his disposition. I want to sense his presence and feel his love. I want to hear Christ when he speaks to me. I want to do what he wants me to do. I want to be what he wants me to be. More than that, I want to hear Christ when he speaks to others. I want to listen, as he speaks to the lost and the saved, to the Jew and the Gentile, and to the Christian and the Muslim. I want to hear what Jesus Christ says as he talks to the committed and to the curious, to the seeker and to the skeptic, to the one who has just discovered him, perhaps just baptized all the way under and up dripping wet, and to the one who is walking away, discouraged and drained.

I want to eavesdrop, as Jesus speaks to you. I want to sit still, as Jesus listens to you. I want to feel his curiosity, his compassion, and his commitment to your wellbeing. I want to watch, as Jesus walks alongside you and behind you and before you, loving you all the way. I want to imitate Jesus, as he *sings with joy and lives with hope.*

I want to know Christ. Because as I know him, I know myself. As I know Jesus, I know my purpose in life. As I know Christ, I embrace the one true ambition for life.

I want to know Christ.

Nineteen

I Press On

But I press on to possess that perfection for
which Christ Jesus first possessed me.
Philippians 3:12

Do you remember Greta Thunberg?

A 15-year-old Swedish girl on the Asperger syndrome spectrum, Greta persuaded her parents to make lifestyle changes. She wanted to reduce their carbon footprint because she was concerned about climate change. Her crusade brought her much attention. In 2018, she was invited to address the United Nations Climate Change Conference. When invited to the United States to speak, she sailed a yacht to North America. Her speech was titled "How Dare You!" and was widely quoted and printed. Speaking on behalf of her generation, she challenged the world to act responsibly. By the end of 2019, when she was only 16, she was named Person of the Year by *Time* magazine.[58]

During that momentous year, she traveled to Rome. In St. Peter's Square, on April 16, she met Roman Catholic Pope Francis. He had just published the most widely read and quoted papal encyclical in Christian history, known by its first words, in Spanish (which

---

[58] See her Wikipedia page for more information about her.

is itself unusual) *Laudato Si'*. He quotes the opening words of the famous "Canticle of the Sun" by Francis of Assisi. It means, "Praise Be to You." That papal document is a strong call to the people of the world to take care of God's creation.

They met, the pigtailed teenager from Sweden and the smiling pontiff from Argentina. The old pope, then 83 years old, said to the young lady, "Go on! Go on! Go on!" He was quoting, intentionally or not, the great apostle himself, who wrote to Francis the Pope, and to Greta the teenager, and to us today, "Press on! I press on" (*Philippians* 3:12).

My message to you today is the same. I press on. You press on. Let us press on.

I.

Providence Church is here today because a few of you made this pledge: "I press on."

Ten years ago, this sanctuary was full to overflowing. Children and babies were everywhere. A choir filled the platform. Money filled the offering plate. And joy filled the souls of all who crowded into these pews. But then conflict and COVID conspired to collapse this wonderful enterprise called Providence. People left, money dried up, and attitudes deteriorated. But some of you said to yourself and to others, "I'm pressing on. I'm not leaving. I will survive the drama and the trauma. God will see us through. I press on."

Can I quote the title of another chapter in this book? "I can do everything [all things] through Christ who strengthens me!"

I am here to speak for all of us new people: Thank you. Thank you for hanging in there. Thank you for praying your way through the trials and tribulations. Thank you for staying when people were transferred out of town, when people relocated to other places, and when people got irritated and looked for greener pastures. Thank you. Thank you for giving, for singing, for leading, for cleaning, for planning, for showing up. Thank you for saying to one another, "I press on!"

Though small in number, we are here now, and we pick up this theme. We press on!

II.

We take our cue from Paul the apostle, written in this warm and wonderful letter that we now call the *Philippians*. He, of all people, had need of resolve.

Paul was in jail somewhere. It was not the first time, and it was not the last time. In fact, the last time led to his death, his martyrdom. But as he dictated this letter to Timothy (as scholars think), he had been jailed by Roman authorities, perhaps some local magistrate or a provincial governor. Local officials like these exercised the ultimate authority from the Roman emperor. They did not like Paul's type: itinerant purveyors of exotic religious nonsense; uprooted disturbers of the peace; quacks and charlatans; and irritants of the first order. Even though he was a Roman citizen, Paul had neither the social standing nor the network of friends to save him from the trials and tribulations of a local jail.

Paul did have people to bring him food and clothes. In this letter, he says "I have all I need." What he meant was that the people of Philippi had sent him what he needed to survive. Jail, then and now, is an unholy place, an unhappy place, and an unhealthy place. It was dangerous. But Paul had this resolve, "I press on!"

Paul had opposition, not only from Roman authorities but also from Jewish leaders. Time and again, his former colleagues were out to get him, out to discredit him, out to contradict his reading of the Torah and his telling of the story of Jesus. Paul took pride in his Jewish heritage, but the Jewish leaders did not take pride in him. He had violated the most basic rules of his tribe, his people, and his religion. He had gone even further than Jesus in criticizing, condemning, and correcting the tradition of patriarchs and prophets and the reasoning of rulers and rabbis. He declared that Jesus is the son of God, risen from the dead, and the judge of all people on the world's last day.

Paul sang a song that his old religionist colleagues did not want to hear:

> Therefore, God elevated Jesus to the place of highest honor and gave him the name above all names; that at the name of Jesus every knee should bow, in heaven and on earth and under the earth, and every tongue declare that Jesus Christ is Lord to the glory of God the Father (2:9-11).

Paul had trouble, not only with Jews but also with his new family of faith. There were plenty of people of The Way, Jesus people, who had no use for Paul. He had many critics inside the church of Jesus Christ. Paul refers to some other Christians as those "who care only for themselves" and "those dogs, those people who do evil, those mutilators who say you must be circumcised to be saved" (3:2).

He may even have had these Christ-claiming critics in mind when he described the "enemies of the cross of Christ" (3:18) who are headed for destruction. Paul had his enemies: in places of imperial power, in places of religious authority, and even in places of Christian confession. Nevertheless, he took as his mantra, "I press on!" He did not quit. He did not surrender. He did not give up. He pressed on. Today, I also will press on, and so should you.

Some of you here today can name the forces arrayed against you: family and friends, for some of you, telling you to give up, to change directions, and to alter your plans; employers and supervisors, for some of you, demanding that you compromise your values, change your schedule, or redo your priorities; neighbors and naysayers, for others of you, pushing you to conform to a way of living that violates your conscience. God says to you today, Press on!

Some of you have no enemies, but you face a rising tide of circumstances, a convergence of factors conspiring against your dreams. You sit sometimes with your head in your hands and mutter to yourself, "I need to quit this foolishness, this unrealistic dream of mine to own my own business, to finish this college degree, to write this book that has been bubbling in my soul for years. I just need to give it all up."

Here is the word of the Lord for you today: Press on! Press on! Press on! Join the great chorus of never-say-die dreamers, and say to yourself, to others, and to God, "I press on!"

III.

When I read Paul's forceful resolve, "I press on," I hear a word our nation needs to hear. The great apostle is writing to the Christian community in the United States. Press on toward the fuller experience of our faith. Press on to the more complete freedom that we envision for all of our people. Press on to possess that for which Christ Jesus first possessed us!

For more than two centuries, we have been working to fulfill the promise of freedom and opportunity for all people. The Civil Rights Movement, led by a brilliant and talented Baptist preacher, Martin Luther King, Jr., focused on the rights of black people in the United States. Our leaders in Washington pushed for equality, integration, and unity in education, housing, employment, and law. I applaud this, even as I am disheartened by the murders of people in Charleston, Minneapolis, Brunswick, and Buffalo. Worse, I am dismayed, even despondent, at the ideology that perpetrated these crimes. It is called "replacement theory"—the notion that too many people of color are pushing white people out of their space, their place of power and privilege, their position of wealth and opportunity. I denounce this evil idea and all of the wickedness that flows out of it.

We need to press on toward liberty and justice for all. White people (and some would say white men!) have controlled everything in this country since Europeans landed in 1492. Look at the mess we are in. We have too many guns, too many people in jail, too much poverty, too much anger, too much hatred, too many people marginalized and stigmatized, and too many people gunned down.

White people need to join hands and hearts with people of all colors to create a more perfect union, to demonstrate that our ideal (as one nation under God) is not merely a slogan or a pledge but the goal toward which we labor. I press on, I say with the ancient apostle.

The Women's Rights Movement, epitomized by the great justice Ruth Bader Ginsburg and others, has labored long and hard for the expanded rights of women: to marry or not to marry, to conceive or not to conceive, to deliver or not to deliver, to study or not to study, to work or not to work, to lead or not to lead, to preach or not to preach, and to judge or not to judge.

I am glad my own daughter was born into a world different from my mother's world. My mother, Reita Redden Moody, was the first person in her family to graduate from college, the first female president of the Baptist Student Union in the Commonwealth of Kentucky, the first female chaplain at the Western Baptist Hospital in Paducah, and among the first to be educated and credentialed as a pastoral counselor. But she was never recognized by the churches or their ministers; she was never ordained by the brethren, and she was told to keep her thoughts to herself.

I honor her. Many here today have followed in her footsteps on that trail others hacked through the wilderness of prejudice and preference. But in some churches today, women cannot even stand in the pulpit. In many churches, women cannot proclaim the Gospel or serve the Lord's Supper.

I say to all of us: "Let's press on!"

There are evil forces at work in our nation: in the legislatures, on the courts, and in the houses of power—religious power and political power. They want to take us back to the world of my mother. I say to all of you, *I am not going back. I am going to press on.*

After the civil rights and women's rights movements, came the gay rights movement. Our nation and our church repented of our sin, changed our mind, our attitude, and our policy, and welcomed the queer community to the table of God. We moved from hostility to hospitality, from judgment to grace, from curse to blessing, and from outcast to honored guest.

We who are followers of Jesus came to imagine that famous painting of Jesus at the last supper, the one by Leonardo of Vinci, redone, with Jesus at the center and the table full of people of all colors, genders, and orientations, young and old, strong and weak, rich and poor, with each serving their neighbor. It is the kingdom of God we have longed to see.

These three changes in American society and the Christian church (civil rights, women's rights, and gay rights) are the result of a movement that is democratic, secular, and spiritual. It is seeking to grant all people the rights and responsibilities of American life guaranteed by our constitution. It is pledging to give to all people the faith, love, and hope of the Christian Gospel. We arrived where we are today because some people took to heart this gospel testimony: "I press on!"

But as this was happening, a reaction set in. Some people were not happy. They did not like integration and equal rights. They did not like women out of the family house and into the state house. They did not like queer neighbors out of the closet and into the limelight. They launched a movement to undo these kingdom advances.

They first captured Christian churches and denominations. Then they captured the Republican Party. They moved on to the capitols and legislatures of state after state. Finally, they seized the White House and the Supreme Court—all in the name of Jesus, of course.

They are not done, these crusaders for the way things used to be. They resist Black Lives Matter. They denounce the right of privacy to women and also the right of public ministry. They are determined to push our brothers and sisters back into the dark closet of condemnation. They are not done. Their numbers are growing, and their intentions are audacious. They marched in Charlottesville. Their people murdered praying people in Charleston and Pittsburgh. One of them walked into the grocery store in Buffalo and murdered ten people. They store up guns and prepare to use them in defense of the way things used to be.

But I am reading the Gospel of God today. I am hearing the word of the Lord today. I am speaking a good word to you today. The words of the Bible in *Philippians* are my words today, "I press on!"

I want to say today that I am not going back. I am not going back to Egypt. I am not going back to segregation, to subjugation, or to silence. I am not going back to the world into which I was born. I am pressing on. I am pressing on to receive the heavenly prize for which God, through Christ Jesus, is calling us.

Let's go together, Providence. Let's press on!

Twenty

I Love You

I love you and long to see you, dear friends,
for you are my joy and the crown I receive for my work.
Philippians 4:1

Just before he died of COVID 19 in 2020, John Prine wrote and privately recorded his last song, "I Remember Everything." Stanza 2 ends with this plaintive and apologetic line, "Sometimes a little tenderness was the best that I could do."[59]

I want to say, sometimes a little tenderness is the very thing we need. Children need it when hurt, and friends need it when suffering. You and I need it when life is heavy and the road is hard. A little tenderness goes a long, long way.

It is a word of tenderness that comes to us today from the hand and heart of the great apostle. "Dear brothers and sisters," he writes, "I love you. I long to see you. Dear friends, you are my joy."

Maybe that is precisely what you need to hear today, from God, from me, or from a treasured friend. Maybe that is precisely what you need to say today: a word of tenderness, of affection, of sweetness, of love. You may need some version of the most wonderful words in human language: "I love you."

---

[59] See footnote 13 above.

I.

Paul is giving us, one phrase at a time, his personal testimony, his life philosophy, and his deepest feelings about what matters. He began with strong resolve: "I never get tired" (3:1). He was talking about his calling in life, his great gospel mission, that which drove him forward. "I consider it trash," he went on to say (3:7). He was thinking about his accomplishments, his resume, the things that once upon a time made him proud and successful and honored. "I want to know Christ," he confessed next (3:10), thinking about the new center of his universe. He was remembering what happened on that road to Damascus when Jesus, the Risen Lord spoke to him; he was reaching down deep to put words to his new vision for life. "I press on," he then writes (3:12), thinking about the hardships, the opposition, and the uncertainties he was facing. God had given him the gift of perseverance, and here he puts it into words. It is a strong and sturdy sentence, one we need to hear now and again.

Then, he comes to this most tender of all testimonies. "I love you." He writes it twice in this one verse (4:1). "Dearly beloved," he says once, and again, "dearly beloved." That is old-fashioned KJV language. Our more modern phrase, "I love you," is deeper, wider, and longer. It goes out gently in all directions: to the head, to the heart, to the memory, to the mind, to the soul, and to the smile. It is the gold card of greetings. It is tenderness at its best.

Paul goes on to add other good words to his testimony. "I praise the Lord" gives voice to the exuberant side of loving God and following Jesus. "I can do everything ... through Christ who gives me strength" is the sure word of spiritual resolve. It grabs hold of the resurrection of Jesus and pulls it into your own soul so that it makes a difference in how you live and love and learn. Finally, Paul testifies, "I have all I need." In our economy of accumulation, this is surely a good gospel word.

In this chapter, we have the best of all worlds, of all words: "I love you"(4:1). It is the fulcrum upon which all else turns. God so loves the world that God filled it with beauty and glory and delight. God so loves the world that God created each of us and gave each of us a name, a face, and a spirit. God so loves you, me, and the stranger across the street that he sent music, art, and dance, and also design, imagination, and emotion of every sort to make this one life a thing of beauty. God so loves you and me and our nearest neighbor that God sent into this world Jesus the Lord, Jesus the savior, Jesus the teacher, Jesus the miracle worker, Jesus the one who sees us when nobody else does, the one who hears us when nobody else does, and the one who loves us when nobody else does.

"Love is a many-splendored thing," the old song says. This even older letter says it as well as any poet or prophet. "I love you," Paul wrote. "You are my joy," he wrote in chapter four, verse one. "You are my beloved," he spelled out in the Greek letters. "I long to see you."

Twice, he uses the strongest, surest, and most spiritual of all words in his own Greek language, *agape*! Love!

II.

It is not just ancient people in Philippi who need a little tenderness, is it? Our community and our country need a little tenderness. We have too much anger, too much irritation, too much accusation for all that goes wrong. The hurting patient bought a gun in Tulsa and went to the hospital, angry at his surgeon that not everything went quite right. He pulled out a rifle and unloaded on everybody. Four people died, including two doctors.

There is a pandemic of violence in our country. Rage is the preferred emotion. Anger and revenge are wreaking havoc on the peace and tranquility of the country. It is a sickness unto death, a disease that goes deep into the soul. We ask each other and ask God, "Is there a balm, a comfort, a healing in Gilead, or Tulsa, or Buffalo, or Hendersonville?"[60]

---

[60] This reference is adapted from *Jeremiah* 8:22.

Yes, it *is* about the guns.

Guns are a killing tool. Guns are implements of violence. Guns are disasters waiting to happen. In the name of Jesus, I denounce them. In the power of the Spirit, I call upon all of us to turn our backs on the gun culture in the United States. The voice of God said to Moses, who stood beside the burning bush with his staff in his hand, "Throw it down, give it up, let it go."[61]

But it is not *just* about the guns. It is about the spirit, the human spirit, and the Holy Spirit. It is about faith, hope, and love. It is about helping instead of hurting, of listening instead of talking, and of smiling instead of snarling. It is about a little tenderness.

It is about putting down the guns and taking up Jesus, the Christ. It is about beating our weapons into plows and our swords into tools. It is about joining a Spirit-filled movement of non-violence, peace, kindness, and that tenderness of which Prine sang and Paul wrote. This is the outpouring of the Holy Spirit that we need today: not the angry, macho, gun-slinging silliness that masquerades as manliness. It is the Jesus stuff, who told his followers to put away their swords, just minutes after kneeling in the garden to pray, "not my will but yours" (*Matthew* 26:42). His death was redemption for the world.

Our former member, Ann Greene, sent me a message yesterday from the First African Baptist Church of Savannah. "I attended this "Swords into Plowshares" event today. It was filmed but I don't know by whom or whether it will be posted.... . Rev. Sharon Risher ... was the keynote speaker. Shane Claiborne with his wife presented the guns into garden tools portion of the program. He is in the background of the blacksmithing picture. The event was well attended."

That needs to become an annual Pentecostal practice. Let's take the lead with that Pentecostal practice here in Henderson County.

---

[61] The story is told in *Exodus* 3. But the version of the story that has the greatest impact on me (and the one that introduced to me this three-fold divine command) is the musical version written and performed by Ken Medema. It is simply entitled "Moses."

III.

There is another way to celebrate the coming of the Holy Spirit. Giving up our guns and moving toward the peaceable kingdom is one way. That may impact your home, our community, and the nation as a whole. It is one way to say, "I love this nation. I love you!" We need thousands of people to practice this sort of *agape* love.

But there is another way to celebrate the coming of the Holy Spirit, and I was reminded of it last week.

A friend from high school called me from her home in Nashville to tell me that Pat Reeder Perkins had died. I felt like the classmate who later wrote on a Facebook page, "This took my breath away." Pat was my friend at church and school. She was attractive, talented, winsome, and disciplined. A graduate of Oklahoma Baptist University with two degrees in music, she later earned a law degree and worked for both the public defender and the state attorney general in Missouri. She married and raised children and lived in Missouri, but for 56 years we talked back and forth. We saw each other occasionally. The last time was four years ago when her choir at the First Baptist Church of Jefferson City came on tour to Savannah, Georgia, just an hour's drive north of my home. She called me to invite me to join them in town for a day and deliver the daily devotional, which I was thrilled to do.

You think you will always have an opportunity to say to somebody "I love you," to write them a note, "You are dear to me," to put your arms around them, look them in the eye and say, "You have been a treasure." I thought I would always have that day to say to my friend Pat, "You have made my life rich and given me reason to praise God."

But it did not happen. Pat was riding in the back seat of a car on vacation with family in Arizona when she slumped back. She never woke up. No warning. No illness. No signs of impending death. A day later, they closed her eyes for good and cremated her body. The next Saturday, late in the afternoon, in Jefferson City, Missouri, we gathered for a celebration of life. I said to her then, in public, what I wished I had said a month earlier, in private.

Pentecost, I remind you, is about what you say, as well as about what you do. Pentecost is a festival of speech. It is allowing the Spirit of God to fill your mouth to overflowing and to bear testimony to the goodness of God and the glory of friendship.

Go home today, and tell somebody, "I love you." Get on the phone today, and tell somebody, "God put you in my life, and I give thanks today." Sit down at your kitchen table today, write a letter like Paul did, and remind somebody of this: "I love you. You fill my life with gladness. I am a stronger, kinder, more Christ-like person because of you."

Then, put on a little John Prine, especially where he sings, "I remember everything…and sometimes a little tenderness is all that I could do." But even that will make it a powerful Pentecostal Sunday.

Twenty-One

I Praise the Lord

How I praise the Lord that you are concerned about me again.
Philippians 4:10

Into the crude and cynical conversation of the American people today, followers of Jesus can speak a chorus of praise, gratitude, and joy. It may be the single most important contribution that believing people can make to public discourse. In so doing, we will be imitating Jesus, our Lord, and also his chief apostle Paul, who wrote to the Philippians this simple testimony, "I praise the Lord."

My message is this: you can choose the negative and complain, or you can choose the positive and rejoice. Let's follow Paul and give thanks to God for all the good in the world and all the blessings in life.

I.

There is much in our country that is not good. We are focused on gun violence every year it seems and hoping for new approaches to keep America safe. We suffered through the worst inflation in more than 20 years. I paid more than $5 a gallon for gas on a recent trip to Missouri. We watched the Congressional hearings of a Big Lie that continues to be told by our former President and embraced by too many of his followers. Every day brings new revelations of sexual abuse and misconduct among religious leaders. Thousands upon thousands of refugees are fleeing poverty and violence and crowding along our southern border. Around all of this, the rising global temperatures give witness to the overarching crisis of the climate.

These things could dominate our minds, much like they dominate the evening news, the cable channels, and the talk shows. They justify some measure of alarm, anger, and angst.

Or, we can turn to other things to feed our souls and shape our speech. We can give thanks for the prosperity of our country, the safety of our travel, and the freedom of our worship. We can celebrate the beauty of the sky, the glory of the national parks, and the birth of our children. We can dance to the music, sing with the choir, and raise our hands in holy happiness.

Some time ago, my grandson, Samuel Wyatt Curson, said to me, "I have decided to be happy in all situations." He was 12 years old, living with his mother, and surviving on a poverty-level income. His is the spirit of Paul, who also chose to be hopeful instead of fearful, joyful instead of jealous, and grateful instead of grumpy. "I praise the Lord" he wrote when he could have just as easily written, "I protest my lot in life." He said, "I am grateful," when he could have said, "I am angry."

Paul had good reason to be grumpy. He was in jail, in a town where he had never been, and far away from most of his family and friends. He was working for a cause—the Jesus Gospel—that was largely unknown and certainly unpopular. He had little evidence of success, other than the few small bands of believing people scattered across the big, bad Roman world. The Jews were against him, the Roman authorities were against him, and even some in his own religious movement were against him. Now and then, he describes this woeful situation. But more often, he ignores it and gives glory to God.

"I praise the Lord" is typical of Paul. It is imbedded in his 8-part testimony, as I have been describing in these chapters. "I never get tired" of the work I am called to do, he says, first. "I consider it trash" he wrote about his pre-Jesus resume. "I want to know Christ" is the way he voiced his deepest passion, ignoring the trouble around him. In fact, in the midst of all that trouble, he writes, "I press on," with a spirit of courage, faithfulness, and perseverance. No wonder he can write to the believers in Philippi, "I love you." When your heart is full of God and your speech is full of Gospel, you can love everyone around you. We are not surprised that through it all, he can sustain this chorus, "I praise the Lord."

II.

I have written above of the funeral of a close friend from the Hazelwood High School class of 1968. She died suddenly, without warning, with no known medical condition. She was 71 years old. That is too young to die. Pat Reeder Perkins was full of talent and energy. Her face carried a ready smile; her voice spoke words of encouragement and gratitude. Her two daughters and 5 grandchildren adored her.

I was one of two speakers at the memorial service. A full choir and orchestra filled the platform, a gospel quartet sang two songs, and 250 people gathered to celebrate her life. We had a choice, did we not? We could bemoan her untimely death. We could grieve her sudden departure, leaving all of us with no time to say good-bye. We could testify to our sorrow.

But we did not. We chose to dwell upon her righteous life and the wide circle of her godly influence. In so doing, we were obeying the Gospel of God, written here in this letter: "Fix your thoughts on what is true, honorable, right, pure, lovely, and admirable. Think about things that are excellent and worthy of praise" (4:8). I amend that text to read: "*Speak* about things that are excellent and worthy of praise."

You have this choice every day. Think, speak, and write about things that are excellent and worthy of praise. You have a choice. Choose praise. Choose joy. Choose gratitude.

All of life and faith is this way. When we pick up the Bible, we can emphasize this verse or that verse. You can read *Psalm* 137, verse 9, "Happy is the one who takes your babies and smashes them against the rocks." Or you can read *Psalm* 136, verse 2, "Give thanks to the God of gods whose faithful love endures forever." We may say "all scripture is given by inspiration of God" (*Second Timothy* 3:16), but today, I will choose the second of these two psalms to guide my thoughts and inspire my praise.

You can read from the epistle we call *First Timothy* where Paul counsels, "Women should learn quietly and submissively. I do not let women teach men or have authority over them. Let them listen quietly" (2:11f). Or you can turn to the roaring letter we know as *Galatians,* where Paul proclaims, "There is neither Jew or Gentile, slave nor free, male nor female. For you are all one in Christ Jesus" (3:28).

It is a matter of emphasis.

Jesus had this same approach to religion. As I wrote in chapter four, one man came to him and asked, "What is the greatest commandment?" In other words, of all the commandments in the Hebrew Bible, which one should we emphasize? Already, Moses had taught the Hebrew people to pay attention to 10 rather than to all 635. We call those the Ten Commandments. Now, one of those readers of the Law of Moses came to Jesus and said, "Which of these should we emphasize the most?"

Jesus did not mention any of the 635 commands in the Torah. Jesus did not even choose any of the Ten given by Moses. He selected two others. He did so by asking a question: What part of the Hebrew Law do you think is most important? The man, well educated, no doubt, said, "Love God with all your heart, soul, mind, and strength." That is the greatest commandment. And the second is this: "Love your neighbor as yourself."[62]

Jesus said, "You are right!" Even Jesus knew that reading the Bible is a matter of emphasis. Are you going to give priority to love and compassion and caring for people? Or, are you going to give priority to judgment, criticism, and keeping score of who is right and who is wrong?

Which do you choose to read and share and celebrate? Are you going to praise the Lord for mercy and grace and love? Or are you going to protest to the Lord and to people about the ugliness and anger and unfairness in the world?

I challenge you today to take up the cause of praise, sing the chorus of gratitude, and raise a joyful noise unto the Lord!

III.

Jesus was a Jew. His followers later came to be called Christians. But Jews and Christians share the same commitment to lift our voices in praise, to give thanks, and to live always grateful for the goodness of life.

We also share values and expectations with Muslims. Yasir Qadhi is dean of the first and only Islamic seminary in North America. It is in the greater Dallas metroplex. In a recent conference, he featured a professor at Southern Methodist University, named Oman Suleiman. I listened to his talk on the first virtue of their believing community. It is found in the opening chapters of the Quran. It is gratitude! The professor spoke for 15 minutes about having gratitude in our souls, gratitude in our voice, and gratitude

---

[62] This story appears in all three synoptic gospels, even though the details differ. In *Matthew* 22:23ff and *Mark* 12:28ff, a Jewish lawyer asks Jesus a question about the greatest commandment, and Jesus answers, naming two. However, in *Luke* 10:25ff, Jesus responds to the lawyer's question with his own question, "What does the law of Moses say? How do you read it?"

in our deeds. His talk about giving thanks could have been given at any gathering of our church!

It is a universal rule of the Spirit: Give thanks. Cultivate gratitude. Rejoice. Praise God. In Judaism, in Christianity, and in Islam, the rule of the Spirit is precisely expressed by Paul when he declares, "I praise the Lord."

Paul was grateful that some friends came to his aid. There is no better feeling than that. When you are in need, you want people to come to your aid. When you are depressed, you want somebody to sit with you and listen to your soul. When you are late in making a payment, you want friends who will lend you money or pay your fee. When you need a ride, you want friends who will go out of their way to pick you up. When you are sick, you want doctors who stay late, employers who give you time off, and a friend who will take you where you need to go and prepare you food when you come home.

My sister once said, "I just want a church where they know my name and will bring me a casserole when I am sick." I say amen to that!

"You have done well," Paul wrote the Philippians, "to share with me in my present difficulty.... You were the only ones who gave me financial help when I first brought you the Good News and then traveled on from Macedonia. No other church did this" (4:14f).

Paul had reason to be thankful, and so do you and I.

Paul had reason to thank God, and so do you and I.

Paul had reason to be grateful, and so do you and I.

In the privacy of your own home or in the public space of a sanctuary, we say with Paul this most fundamental confession of faith, "I praise the Lord."

Twenty-Two

I Can Do All Things

For I can do everything through Christ, who gives me strength.
Philippians 4:13

During the 2021 baseball season, Pittsburgh Pirate third baseman, Ke'Bryan Hayes, hit a home run. It was a Tuesday night home game against the Los Angeles Dodgers in PNC Park. It was part of a stellar rookie year for the 22-year-old star, except for this fact: he failed to touch first base. The umpire ruled him out!

It is important that we touch all four bases in this text (4:13): One, I can! Two, do all things! Three, through Christ! And four, who strengthens me!

If we can perfect this spiritual practice, we will enjoy peace in our inner spirit, experience impact through our gospel work, and receive "the heavenly prize to which God, through Christ Jesus, is calling us" (4:13).

I.

First base: I can! We can!

What is not to like about this can-do spirit? I like people who say, "I can get that done." I have some of that in me. Any time people say to me, "That can't be done!" I don't believe them. I know that sometimes they are right but not always. From sailing around the world to discovering the human genome, from bringing a church back from the edge to granting equal rights to LGBTQ people, I am one to say: Yes, we can! Yes, I can!

In 2021, June 19 became a federal holiday. It happened because 89-year-old Opal Lee decided to make it her mission. She started walking from her home in Ft. Worth, Texas, to Washington, D.C., to deliver signed petitions. She said, "Yes, I can!" As she walked across Georgia, I had the opportunity to interview her on TheMeetingHouse.[63] I was not taught about Juneteenth, Galveston, and General Order #3. I doubt that any of you were taught that piece of history. But thanks to a woman who had this "I can" attitude, our grandchildren will know.

Paul must have been this kind of forceful personality: full of optimism rather than pessimism, full of confidence rather than confusion, and full of determinism rather than doubt. This was his natural disposition, long before his conversion to Jesus. This gave him the audacity to try to stamp out the Christian movement and to demand authority to travel to Damascus to arrest any of the Jewish community who were followers of the heretical rabbi, Jesus of Nazareth.

Paul took that same supreme confidence into his work as an apostle, a missionary, an apologist, a preacher, an organizer, a writer, and a follower of Jesus. He never hesitated to say, "Yes, I can!" But this natural ability was baptized by his faith in Jesus and his calling from God.

---

[63] The podcast of my conversation with her is available on my website, TheMeetingHouse. net/podcasts.

II.

Second base: I can do all things!

I can do all things! What in the world did Paul mean? We already know there were things Paul could not do. For instance, he could not put a stop to the Jesus movement of his day. He tried and failed. He could not resist the calling of God and the commission from Jesus. They confronted him, and he could not resist them. Paul could not master his own self. Isn't this what he meant when he wrote in his most famous of all letters, (to the Roman church) that "the good that I want to do, I can't; and the evil that I desire to avoid, I can't. Who will deliver me from this body of death?" (7:15-16). In another poignant passage, he confesses that he prayed three times for his disability—whatever it was—to be gone, lifted, removed; but, apparently, it never was, leaving Paul to claim God's grace as sufficient to sustain him (*Second Corinthians* 12:8-10).

Yes, there were many things that Paul could not do!

He could not put to silence his detractors. He could not protect himself against the authorities who constantly put him in jail. He could not deliver himself from jail.

Paul resigned himself to death. He wrote in one letter, "I am ready to be poured out like an offering. I have run the course and finished the race" (*Second Timothy* 4:6-7). Tradition tells us that, eventually, Paul was martyred for Christ, unable to free himself to finish his work.

What *was* on his mind when he wrote, "I can do all things"? He was not superman, able to leap tall buildings, stop speeding trains, or move faster than a speeding bullet. Superman was a fantasy, then and now. Paul was not a superman, not a super Christian, and not a super apostle.

What did Paul mean when he said, "I can do all things"?

III.

Third Base. Through Christ!

Paul connected his ambition, his personality, and his intellect with Jesus, the Risen Lord. It was Jesus Christ who enabled him to find the meaning of his own supreme ability and confidence. In Christ, Paul found his strength and his mission. He was confident of doing all that God called him to do. All of his considerable ambition was now funneled through Jesus. All of his immense intelligence was surrendered to Jesus, the Risen Lord. All of his rare organizing and managing ability was put at the feet of Jesus.

My middle son is intelligent and talented, but he has had a terrible time navigating life. He got into trouble with just about everything capable of disrupting life. Sometimes, I have thought to myself, "He has everything … just not quite enough Jesus!" Jesus has the power to channel his intelligence, his talent, and his ambition to make them kingdom worthy, gospel worthy, and life worthy. Jesus can do the same for you.

Early in his life, Paul (as Saul) had this problem. He had been going in one direction: religious, disciplined, focused, but also judgmental, controlling, and violent. Now, he is going in another direction, because that is the way Jesus Christ leads: humble, patient, helpful, gracious, and full of love. Years later, he wrote, "Even if I speak with the tongues of angels and orators, but do not love, I am nothing, I accomplish nothing, I succeed at nothing. If I understand all the mysteries and prophecies and doctrines, but have not love, I am a gong, a noise, mere silliness, an emptiness, wasted, wanting" (*First Corinthians* 13:1-2, paraphrased).

Paul found that love in Jesus, the crucified and risen Lord. His testimony is this: I bend my knee at the foot of the cross. I surrender what I have to Jesus. I accept his lordship, his mission, his methods, his schedule, his ways, and his spirit.

How we need this in our world today!

Today, too many people are renouncing the prince of peace and taking up the weapons of war. The Christian Patriarch of Moscow is renouncing the faith by endorsing the Russian invasion of Ukraine. People are dying, homes are exploding, and the leader of the Russian Orthodox Church is granting his blessing to all of it.

In our own country, people are taking their tools and making them into weapons. They are giving up their plows, rakes, and shovels and transforming them into pistols, rifles, and shotguns. They are trading tool belts for high-capacity magazines that fire 60 bullets a minute. They are solving problems by pulling out pistols. Gun sales are up from 10 million a year, only a quarter century ago, to 40 million a year now. People are arming themselves with the weapons of the world instead of the breastplate of righteousness, the helmet of salvation, and the sword of the spirit.

Because of Christ Jesus, Paul turned his back on violence and death and took up the cause of non-violence and life, of service and compassion. Before his conversion, he was the one arresting and charging people; after his conversion, he was the one arrested and prosecuted. Before his conversion, Paul depended upon the power of Roman law, authority, and prison bars; after his conversion, he depended upon love, truth, and the persuasive power of personal testimony. "I was lost, but Jesus found me," he would say. Jesus can find you also and bring you to a place of peace and trust, to a place of kindness and generosity.

"I can do all things" through the ways and means of Christ, through the power of the Gospel of love and service, and through the call to conversion and the consecrated life.

Don't look to armies and armaments to do the work of God. Don't arm yourself with the weapons of this world. Put on the whole armor of God. Take up faith, and hope, and love, and do the work God has called you to do.

IV.

"I can do all things through Christ who gives me strength."

Here is home plate, the piece of this spiritual puzzle that puts everything into place. We need strength, some kind of strength, a strength to get us through the day and the year, to make us strong enough to meet the challenges that face us, to keep us hopeful instead of despondent, and to keep us loving the people who disrespect us.

Providence people recently stood around the table at the local Pride Picnic. I was proud to be there. On my Facebook feed is a regular roll of pictures from others who participated in Pride events this week and this month. In identifying with them, I was with a community that, 10 years ago or 25 years ago, would have been difficult for me to embrace.

I remember clearly an important episode on my journey with the LGBTQ community. I had just taken the job of dean of the chapel at Georgetown College. My office was on the ground floor of the chapel. One day, a senior administrator knocked on my door. "Can I talk to you?" he asked. He came in and closed the door behind him and sat down. "I have been watching you and listening to you," he said, referring to my role leading the chapel services at the college. "I think I can trust you. I want to tell you something," he continued. He proceeded to tell me his story: college graduate, married with children, church member and Sunday School teacher, and fundraiser at the college. "All of that will crumble," he said, "when I tell people I am gay."

I did not know what to say. He did not need me to say anything. He just needed me to listen and keep my mouth shut—which is what I did. And when he finally came out, he lost all of it: his job, his family, his church, and his friends.

At times like these, we both needed that phrase, "through Christ who gives me strength." He needed strength to navigate life and survive the pressure. I needed strength to stay by his side and understand what was happening. That was 25 years ago, when I was embedded in the conservative Christian Baptist culture of the American South. I knew that my friend was in a process of change, and I knew that I was in a process of change. "Conversion" is what we call it in the religion business. Here was an illustration of the common assertion: it is the church (and her ministers) who need to change.

During that Pride Picnic, I stood and listened to the hecklers across the street. Their rants of judgment and danger interrupted our gospel work of listening, loving, and laughing. There were about ten of them, with placards and a PA system. They passed the microphone from one person to another, trying to drown out our happiness with their hurtful version of the Gospel. Time and again, one of their preachers would call our name, Providence Baptist Church, and denigrate our mission and damn our message.

I asked myself this question: Who needs the conversion here? Who needs a change of heart? What is the strength of Christ trying to do here, on this lovely day in the public park? What is the one thing that is happening today?

The big thing is always the conversion of our own hearts, our own lives, our own actions. I can do all things through Christ, who convicts me of my prejudice and ignorance and indifference. I can do all things through Christ, who converts me from my own ambitions and my own anxieties. I can do all things through Christ, who comforts me in the midst of my mistakes and my misjudgments. I can do all things through Christ, who strengthens me on the journey to faith, hope, and love. I can do all things through Christ, who strengthens me to confess my sins and straighten my walk and embrace a gospel witness in this angry, anxious world. I can do all things through Christ, who strengthens me to love everybody, serve everybody, and welcome everybody. I can do all things through Christ who strengthens me to *sing for joy and live with hope.*

Twenty-Three

I Have All I Need

At the moment, I have all I need-and more!
I am generously supplied with the gifts you sent me.
Philippians 4:18

This sentence by the great apostle may be the most counter-cultural statement of this entire letter. It strikes us as so out of place in our culture of accumulation. Not an hour goes by without an encouragement to buy more of what we have or don't have. This Tuesday is Prime Day. It is the day those with Amazon Prime membership can save big time with only one condition: you spend money! Like Black Friday in November, Prime Day is Spend-a-Buck-Day (to take the name of a Kentucky Derby winner from 1985). Into the frenzy of buying and selling, the word of God speaks to us today in this simple, powerful statement of faith: "I have all that I need."

I.

Let's review Paul's situation. He was an itinerant evangelist for a small, marginalized religion, much like Sikhism is today. He never mentions family. He did have a trade, we learn elsewhere—tentmaking

(*Acts of the Apostles* 18:3). But he did not seem to own property or equipment or even supplies. He was a member of no organization: no trade union, no chamber of commerce, no running or biking club, and no community organization. In other words, he had none of the social or professional amenities that we associate with citizenship or community or neighborhood.

In a letter later in life, he mentioned his manuscripts and his coat (*Second Timothy* 4:13). So, he must have had a few things, but he was poor. There is a much longer list of things he did not have. Paul did not have a gun, or a sword, or (probably) not even a knife. Yes, he used these images of armor to write something true about the spiritual life. Put on the breastplate of righteousness. Take the helmet of salvation. Pick up the sword of the spirit. (See *Ephesians* 6:13-17). But there is no evidence that he ever carried a sword, or a gun, let alone a military style assault rifle.

Paul owned no home, no house, not even a storage shed somewhere around the Mediterranean. How he could move from country to country without at least a storage shed, I'll never know. He did not own a summer cottage, or an RV, or even a tent (even though he was a tentmaker by trade). He did not have an iPhone, a laptop, or even a pager. And he had no GPS!! How did he survive? Here is one clue: no passwords. I, on the other hand, had to buy a phone just to store page after page of passwords that I am required to maintain just to live and stay connected in the United States.

Paul, the apostle, had none of the things that we think are essential to life. Nevertheless, he writes, "I have all that I need."

What in the world *did* he have?

II.

First, Paul had food. Frankly, that's what this whole letter is about—food. Epaphroditus delivered food and money from the congregation at Philippi. In the Roman system, an incarcerated person was not fed by the jailer or the authorities. He or she depended upon those on the outside—family, friends, strangers, vendors—to provide food. Over and over in this letter, Paul expresses gratitude for these provisions. When he writes, "I have all I need," he is no doubt thinking first about food.

It is stunning how central food is to religion. Food was at the center of the ministry of Jesus. He ate with saints and sinners, the gospels tell us. He fed thousands of people. He said, "I am the bread of life" (*Gospel of John* 6:35). What did he give us to remember him? A meal! Yes, I know it has been transformed into a stripped-down ceremonial ritual. We have to fight our way through layers of tradition to get back to the original gift: a meal. "Eat this bread and remember me. Drink this cup, all of you," Jesus said, as reported in some fashion in all the gospels.

One of the funniest cartoons I have seen lately is the one showing what DaVinci's Last Supper painting would look like if the Baptists had been involved. It would feature not only a loaf of bread and a cup or two of wine, but also casseroles and salads, sliced ham and deviled eggs, pies and cakes, and here and there plastic containers straight out of the kitchen cabinet, full of potato salad or meat loaf. Frankly, that is more like it! That is the Lord's Supper! That is the communion of the saints. That is the bread of life. That is the food for which Paul was thankful.

Second, Paul had friends. Over and over in this little letter, Paul expresses his appreciation to his friends for their support, their generosity, and their loyalty. He mentions three of them: Timothy, Epaphroditus, and Clement. He mentions those who helped him earlier in Philippi. *Acts of the Apostles* tells a story about that (16:11-15). Lydia had heard Paul preach and teach and pray and was pulled into his circle of friends. Some think that she was his chief benefactor.

Everybody needs friends. You don't need many, but you do need some. You need people to check on you when you are sick, to visit you in the hospital, to invite you out to eat every now and then, to write you a Christmas card and a birthday card, and to remember the important days in your life. The pandemic has pushed us apart, and now gun violence is making us wary of going out to watch a parade, run a race, or even attend church.

Some of the great songs of the last 50 years celebrate friends: Simon and Garfunkel singing "Bridge over Troubled Water," James Taylor singing, "You've Got a Friend," and all of us singing with Bill Withers, "Lean on Me." These are anthems of friendship. There is no reason why we can't sing them in church. What a friend we have in Jesus, yes, but what a friend we have in each other.

You have heard me say this before. When people come into our sanctuary or into any sanctuary or even to any prayer circle or picnic gathering, they are subconsciously asking themselves, "Can I be friends with these people?"

When Paul wrote these wonderful words, "I have all I need," he was thinking of his friends.

Paul had plenty of food and enough friends, but he also had a deep and abiding faith. Paul had few material things, but he had an enormous supply of spiritual things—faith. He believed in the unseen power of God. At the end of our gatherings on Wednesday nights, which we called Deeper, we departed with these words of blessing: "Let your light so shine that people might see the goodness and grace that fills the universe and give glory to the One who created, sustains, and redeems all things." This is an expression of our faith.

Faith, the writer to the *Hebrews* asserts in our Bible (11:1), is the evidence of things unseen. We believe that unseen forces are all around us: love that flows from person to person, trust that animates our common work, hope that keeps us going when bad things happen, and joy that fills our voices and our souls. Wrap those three together, and what you have is faith.

It is faith that will get you through tough times. Paul was having what we call a tough time. Work was slow. Success was thin. Times were hard. Prison walls were thick. But Paul had faith in God, faith in his future, faith in his work, and faith in the unseen streams of grace swirling all around him.

During the summer of 2022, in Highland Park, Illinois, a terrible thing happened. A lone gunman took to the rooftop and opened fire. Seven people were killed, and dozens were wounded. It was horrific. But in such circumstances, it is common to hear survivors say, "I have faith. We will get through this. We have faith in God. I don't know what I would do without my faith."

What they mean is that by faith, I connect to the unseen God who strengthens us, comforts us, heals us, and lifts us up. Yes, there is much in this world to drag us down: physical things, dangerous things, inner things, secret things. But, "through it all, I've learned to trust in Jesus! I've learned to trust in God." Isn't that the lyric to a song?[64]

III.

Paul had all he needed. He had food set before him, he had friends who attended to his needs, and he had a faith in the purposes of God in the world. I can say with Paul, "I have all I need." Can you say that? If you don't have enough food, let us know; we will help you. If you don't have friends, reach out around you; we will be your friends. If you don't have faith in the living God, open your heart today: trust God, lean on Jesus, and walk in the Spirit.

I have all I need. But I am here today to testify for you, too. We have all we need. We have a small congregation, but we have a large heart. We have a makeshift broadcast apparatus, but we have faithful folk who listen and watch each week. We have a modest budget, but we have what we need to maintain our buildings, pay our leaders, and send support to Cuba and Ukraine. We have two buildings, neither very large, but they are sufficient to allow us to worship and feed a roomful of people each Sunday afternoon. We

---

[64] Yes, it is! "Through It All" written and sung by Andrae Crouch.

have a brief history—just since 2001—but we trust in our future because we have confidence in the God who called us into being and who sustains our gospel ministry.

We don't have much, but we have all we need. Thanks be to God!!

Twenty-Four

The Rest of God's People

All the rest of God's people send you greetings, too,
especially those in Caesar's household.
May the grace of the Lord Jesus Christ be with your spirit.
Philippians 4:21-23

"Jeremiah was a bullfrog," we sang many years ago with Three Dog Night. But Jeremiah was also a prophet of the highest order. He lived centuries before Jesus, during a time of political intrigue and religious confusion in ancient Israel. His most famous sermon is recorded in chapter 7 of the book of Jeremiah. It is his lone voice of warning against the peace-promising messages of other prophets and priests. Neither the people nor their king knew who was speaking the truth—those who were preaching peace, or Jeremiah, who was warning of danger.

Later, King Zedekiah imprisoned Jeremiah on false charges. The brave prophet of God told the king and his minions that the armies of Babylon would defeat Israel. But on the sly, the king sent for the prophet with the minority voice, with the unpopular opinion, and with the word that stood in sharp contrast to the religious leaders who ran the temple.[65]

"Is there any word from the Lord?" the king asked Jeremiah.

"Yes, there is," Jeremiah replied to Zedekiah. "Babylon will crush you."

It is not always easy to know who speaks the truth, who speaks for God, who speaks the Word of the Lord.

In America, voices clammer for attention, many of them claiming to speak for God, for the Church, and for Jesus. For decades, one group of vocal and persistent voices has sounded out in the name of God, especially on the issue of life, abortion, and health care. That group—some Catholics and some Evangelicals—has gained a larger microphone and announced to the world what they think is the word of the Lord. They were responding to the June 2022 Supreme Court decision on privacy and abortion, *Dobbs v. Jackson Women's Health Organization* in June of 2022.

But I am here today to give voice to the rest of God's people. I am here with Jeremiah to push back, to beg to differ, and to speak a word that stirs up opposition. I am here to say that there is another way to love God, live in the spirit, and follow Jesus.

Once again, I take my inspiration from Paul's letter, *Philippians*.

I.

Not everybody looks at the Gospel in the same way or from the same place, asking the same questions. This is why, from the very beginning of the Christian movement, we have had many options, many voices, and many leaders, all claiming to march at the head of the Jesus parade. We struggle with that now in the United States: Who speaks for God?

---

[65] The story is told in *Jeremiah* 27. It is one of the most dramatic scenes in the biblical narrative, just as Jeremiah's famous Temple Sermon, found in chapter 7, is one of the most powerful sermons or speeches in the Bible.

Paul struggled with that in the ancient Mediterranean world. In chapter one of *Philippians*, he wrote about his work and about the work of others. "Some preach out of jealousy and rivalry ... . They preach with selfish ambition ... . They want to make my chains more painful for me" (1:15, 17).

It is an old strategy to challenge the motives of those who do not like us, who do not agree with us, and who do not support us. We respond by casting doubt on their personhood, on their judgment, or on their motives. Paul had to defend himself all the time, even as he sometimes spoke disparagingly of others.

He goes on to write, "Don't be intimidated by your enemies" (1:18). Who are these enemies: the magistrates who arrested him or other apostles who disparaged him? In chapter two, he writes about Timothy, "I have no one else like Timothy. He genuinely cares about your welfare. All the others care only for themselves and not for what matters to Christ" (2:21).

Here again, Paul pushes back against other disciples, other evangelists, and other apostles. There is a tussle going on in Philippi for the loyalty of the Philippian people.

Then, Paul turns to name-calling: "Watch out for those dogs!" (3:2). He is referring to other Christian teachers who emphasized circumcision. They criticized Paul because he did not require it. Here is the first big division of the house in Christian history: what to do with the Gentiles—how can they become followers of Jesus? Some contended that they must be circumcised; others, including Paul, said, No.

This same kind of tension runs throughout the gospels. Remember when the disciples wanted to call down fire from heaven? But Jesus said, No! Then on the mount of transfiguration, some disciples wanted to build altars or memorials. Again, Jesus said, No! At Caesarea Philippi, Jesus asked his disciples, "Who do the people say I am?" They answered, "Some say Elijah. Some say a prophet. But we say you are Messiah." (See *Matthew* 16:18-20.) Even among these followers of Jesus, there were different ideas, different interpretations, and different voices.

The great council in Jerusalem, described in *Galatians* 2 and *Acts of the Apostles* 15, pits the influence of James, the brother of Jesus, against Simon Peter, the chief among the apostles. Even at that early stage of Christian history, there were divisions of the house, contrary voices, and opposing thoughts.

It is easy to say that *this* is the way, *this* is the word, or *this* is what Jesus wants. But it has been a problem all along.

On every issue in the history of American Christianity, the voices come from every direction: on slavery and abolition; on alcohol, abstinence, and temperance; on baptism, immersion, and sprinkling; on women, leadership and ordination; on sexuality, orientation and hospitality; on speaking in tongues and the fullness of the Spirit; and on bishops, pastors, overseers, and elders. On every issue, there are voices and voices, all invoking Jesus and God and the Holy Spirit, all quoting scripture, and all claiming the blessing from on high.

The Bible calls us to discern the spirits, and we try to do that. Paul tells us to ignore some teachers, and some we are glad to ignore. As I wrote in chapter eight, one tent preacher announced to his congregation, in Nashville, that God had revealed to him that there were 6 witches in his congregation, some of whom he claimed were under the tent, sitting and listening to him as he preached. I know craziness when I hear it, sometimes! But often I wonder: is she speaking the truth? Is he reading things right?

Don't you ever feel like this? Do you ever wonder, whom should I believe or follow or embrace? What about that Moody guy? What's he talking about? Is he for real?

III.

The loudest voices in the American religious world are currently celebrating. Roman Catholic leaders, from Pope Francis to parish priests everywhere, gave thanks for the Supreme Court ruling on abortion. The U. S. Conference of Catholic Bishops declared that "the pro-life movement deserves to be numbered among the great movements for social change and civil rights in our nation's history."[66] The 6 justices who issued the decision are all Catholic.

Louder still are the words of the white Evangelical leaders. The president of the Southern Baptist Convention announced the support of his denomination for the new ruling. The president of the National Association of Evangelicals praised the anti-abortion decision of the Supreme Court. Millions of pew-sitting Christians in churches of all types have worked to this end, and they are celebrating today. They are celebrating, not because America has changed its mind or practice, but because they finally secured 6 of *their* people on the Supreme Court.

But I speak today on behalf of what Paul called "the rest of God's people."

There are millions of us. We treasure the right to privacy. We support the need for women to have body autonomy. We think that this Supreme Court decision is a rude intrusion of a religious ideology into the personal decision-making of people and into the democratic processes of the United States.

In recent decisions, the Supreme Court has demonstrated what minority rule looks like. A majority of Americans favor the right to choose. A majority also favor stricter gun laws. Most Americans support the separation of church and state. But this week, 6 justices announced the end of privacy, the expansion of gun rights, and did serious damage to that wall of separation. Fifty years of preaching, praying, and protesting have not convinced a majority of the American people that a ban on abortion is a gospel imperative.

Today, from pulpits, pews, and prayer circles all over the country, we, the dissenters from these Court decisions, send our gospel greeting to the nation. We declare that religious ideology

---

[66] See the statement on the website of the United States Conference of Catholic Bishops, dated June 24, 2022 (www.usccb.org/news)

should not dominate public policy. We assert that tax dollars should not support the teaching in religious schools. We contend that surrendering guns, rather than brandishing guns, is inspired by the life and teaching of Jesus.

I want to be frank today. I am not promoting abortion as a Christian practice. I treasure life and birth and living to the glory of God. But the Catholic position on this matter rules out abortion *and* contraception. Already, some in high places are calling for the Court to overturn their 1965 Supreme Court ruling known as *Griswold vs Connecticut* that confirmed the freedom to use contraception.

I likewise dissent from the Evangelical position on life. It is often described as supporting the right to life from conception to birth, but after that, mother and baby are on their own. They claim this supports a "right to life." But these same white Evangelicals are the religious group most likely to own guns, support capital punishment, and go to war—hardly a pro-life agenda!

Hear a word from the rest of God's people, as Paul describes his own cohort. Keep judges and prosecutors out of the doctor's office. Keep our tax money away from religious schools. Keep your gun locked up in a safe place. Or, as Johnny Cash used to sing, "Don't take your guns to town, boys, don't take your guns to town." You remember, don't you? Guns were the issue when Wyatt Earp and his brothers confronted the Clanton gang at the OK Corral in 1881. In those days in Tombstone, Arizona, the rule was this: turn your guns in to the sheriff if you want to come to town.

Haven't those justices watched the movie, *Tombstone?*

IV.

The rest of God's people know that there is a bigger threat ahead. We only need to read the Supreme Court majority opinion of Clarence Thomas and remember what happened after the Civil War. That war granted freedom to millions of enslaved people. The federal government initiated a program of support and protection for the freed slaves. It was known as Reconstruction. It had great ambitions to pull the once-enslaved people into the mainstream of American life: living, praying, voting, working, owning, traveling, loving, raising families, and serving as public officials. It was a time filled with idealism and optimism. The future was not to be like the past.

But then the reaction set in.

The white masters seized control of the levers of power. Powerful financial, legal, political, and religious interests pushed back against this wave of freedom. They launched the revenge of the conservatives, who wanted nothing to do with the progress on civil and human rights. They legalized segregation, put blacks into their own ghettos and their own schools, restricted where they could walk and talk, live and work, and undid most of what the Civil War and subsequent legislation had won. To enforce their new but old regime, they even embraced the practice of lynching.

There is a new museum in Montgomery, Alabama, commemorating the history of lynching in the United States. Today, there is also a movement designed to roll back all the civil and human rights progress of the last 70 years. It is not just abortion these celebrating citizens have in mind, but contraception, women's rights, interracial marriage, gay and lesbian rights, voting rights, immigrant rights, and human rights. Financial interests, legal interests, political interests, and religious interests—all conspire today to push back against the future of the United States. Our future is brown, and diverse. It is religious and secular; it is Christian and Muslim and Nothing at all.

Miss Liberty still lifts her lamp beside the golden door. It is a door that leads to equality, opportunity, freedom, and dignity for each and every person. But some people don't like this. They deny building permits to mosques. They deny ballots to the poor. They deny access to the refugee. They deny freedom to the LGBTQ community.

"Stony the road we trod," we sang last week in that great anthem of black freedom.[67] The road ahead got a lot stonier this week: not just for people of color but for all of us who value equality, freedom, and dignity. Today's right-wing Supreme Court launched the revenge of the conservatives. They ripped a hole in the wall of separation and blew up a fundamental right for women, while expanding the gun-slinging rights of men.

We have a long, stony road ahead of us. But here is a good word, a good gospel word from the rest of God's people, and I echo the very last words of this wonderful letter:

May the grace of the Lord Jesus Christ be with your spirit, as we struggle to maintain the separation of church and state. May the grace of the Lord Jesus Christ be with your spirit, as we reassert the inalienable right to privacy. May the grace of the Lord Jesus Christ be with your spirit, as we surrender our weapons on the altar of the God of peace. May the grace of the Lord Jesus Christ be with your spirit, as we *sing for joy and live with hope.*

---

[67] "Lift Every Voice and Sing," sometimes called the Black National Anthem, written and composed by brothers James Weldon Johnson and J. Rosamond Johnson.

Twenty-Five

The Good News of God

*I will know that you are standing together
with one spirit and one purpose,
fighting together for the faith, which is the Good News.*
Philippians 1:27

Robert Bratcher grew up living with missionary parents in Brazil. He came to the United States to attend college and in 1941—more than 80 years ago—graduated from Georgetown College in Kentucky. He studied Greek in college, seminary, and graduate school, and went to work for the American Bible Society.

Dr. Bratcher was the lead translator of the most widely distributed modern English translation of the New Testament.[68] In 1966, it was known as *Good News for Modern Man*. By 1976, he had finished supervising a similar translation of the Old Testament. Now, it is more commonly known as the *Good News Bible* or *Today's English*

---

[68] I know of no clear reference substantiating this assertion! A few years ago, I investigated the question. I reviewed available publication and sales records of many modern translations. When combining such statistics for all versions of the testament first known as *Good News for Modern Man*, they easily exceeded those of other translations, such as *The Living Bible*, the *New International Version*, the *English Standard Version*, even *The Message*. This is probably because the American Bible Society gave away so many without cost and sold so many for such a meager price.

Version. Dr. Bratcher died in 2010, in Chapel Hill, North Carolina, at the age of 90.[69]

I often use a second edition of that testament, one owned by my father, G. T. Moody. From that version, I quote from *Philippians* 1:27 and take as my text today: "Now, the important thing is that your manner of life be as the Gospel of Christ requires, so that, whether or not I am able to go to see you, I will hear that you stand firm with one common purpose, and fight together with only one wish, for the faith of the Gospel."

It is interesting to note that, of the 8 places in this short letter where this Greek word *euangelion* appears, it is translated "gospel" 7 times and "good news" once. Chapter 4, verse 15, reads in the *Good News Bible*, "You Philippians yourselves know very well that when I left Macedonia, in the early days of preaching the good news, you were the only church to help me."

Today, I ask this question: What is the good news?

I.

What is the Good News?

I first searched for an answer to this question in the Bible. I began with Jesus. I started with the story of Jesus, written in *Mark*. "Gospel," is a category of literature, like novel or autobiography. Immediately, the word *gospel* means both a message and a literature.

Here is Mark's summary statement. "Later on, after John was arrested, Jesus went into Galilee, where he preached the God's Good News. 'The time promised by God has come at last,' he announced, 'The kingdom of God is near! Repent of your sins and believe the Good News!'" (1:15).

Jesus said (and here I paraphrase and expand), "Here is good news: the reign of God is near, the rule of God is around the corner, the kingdom of God is about to break into human history." His disciples

---

[69] See note 16.

restated it like this: "We killed Jesus. God raised him from the dead." Those first disciples had their own way of stating the good news!

The message of Jesus is this: the kingdom of God is near! But the Gospel *from* Jesus later became the Gospel *about* Jesus. The disciple, Simon Peter, stood up on the day of Pentecost and said, "You killed Jesus by letting sinful men nail him to the cross. But God raised him from the dead... ." (*Acts of the Apostles* 2:23-24).

Later, Paul, the apostle, could write, in the famous chapter fifteen of *First Corinthians*, "I passed on to you what was most important and what had also been passed on to me. Christ died for our sins.... He was buried, and he was raised to life on the third day...." (15:3ff).

But as we read the Bible, we might hear others give their own version of the Good News. To Moses, the good news was, "I will let your people go to freedom." To Hannah, the good news was, "You will have a child." To David, the good news was, "You will be king of Israel." To Isaiah, the good news was, "A light will shine in the darkness." To the psalmist, the good news was, "God forgives our sin, heals our diseases, rescues us from death, and crowns us with loving kindness." To Matthew, the good news was the words of the angel who said to Joseph, "Do not fear to take Mary as your wife." To Mary and Martha, the good news was, "Lazarus is alive!" To Zacchaeus, the good news was "Salvation came to my house." To John, in exile on the isle of Patmos, the good news was that the new Jerusalem will descend from heaven to earth, and a river of life will flow from it to nourish the tree of life and provide leaves for the healing of the nations.

Paul, in *Philippians*, quotes the early Christian hymn (2:5-11, and here I paraphrase). It is a celebration of the Good News: "Christ was by very nature God. He took the humble position of a slave and was born as the man Jesus. Jesus humbled himself, even to the death on the cross. But God raised him from the dead and gave hm a name above all names. And one day all will proclaim Jesus Christ as Lord, to the glory of God the father." This is the anthem of good news. This is the gospel song sung by those first followers of Jesus.

II.

In these biblical examples, God is present in the dire circumstances, bringing life from death, victory from defeat, hope from despair, love from hate, and reconciliation from alienation. It is the resurrection power of God, exerting itself in every circumstance of life.

This echoes in what Paul wrote in our letter: "I want to know Christ and the power of his resurrection." The *New Living Translation* states it this way: "I want … to experience the mighty power that raised Jesus from the dead" (3:10).

This is the power that brings babies to childless couples, that anoints the least likely to be the leader, that frees the slave and transforms the enslaver, that forgives our sin and rescues us from death. This is the power that does more than we ask or think, that converts the sinner and changes the critic, that frees the addict and converts the racist, that makes a person both wealthy and generous, and that opens our eyes to see the naked who need to be clothed, the hungry who need to be fed, and the stranger who needs a friend.

This is resurrection power, the power of the living God that created the world, raised Jesus from the dead, and will one day make a new heaven and a new earth.

Jesus is alive. God is present. Spirit is moving. Miracle is possible. Life is good. We sing with the psalmist, "Bless the Lord, O my soul and all that is within me, bless your holy name" (103:1 KJV).

I have a friend in Gainesville, Florida. He and his wife were in college with me.[70] He just retired after a long and distinguished career as a minister and pastor. Like me, he has a son who has struggled with addiction. His name is Andrew. He left his family, fled to Ohio, and ended up in Asheville, North Carolina, all driven by his addiction.

What is the Gospel to such a person?

---

[70] Rev. Dr. Greg and Karen Magruder.

Andrew posted this on his Facebook page:

One more day, one step closer. Almost two months sober. Thank you, Lord. Sobriety is tough, tougher than I would have ever imagined. But it is not as tough as wearing the mask behind addiction and saying everything is Okay. The nights I spent alone drinking myself to sleep while I cried because I hurt so badly or the days I would go without sleep because staying high suffocated my inner self crying out for help. I was a fool, a man of folly, a coward, wicked and wretched, seeking the approval of worldly peers, while my father in heaven turned his face in shame because He knew he had great things in store for me. 60 days. 60 days of walking the path God has been waiting for. 60 days of showing me his love and compassion for his prodigal son's return. 60 days I have been a light to this dark world of addiction. My next 60 days will show the glory of God and his wonderful blessing he graciously floods upon my life. But just for today, I'll take it one step at a time, with my head held high and walk side by side with Christ.

This is the good news to an addict, that Jesus Christ, the risen Lord, walks side by side with us, through addiction and denial, around tragedy and trauma, over failure and frustration, and in the midst of grief and loss. Jesus died, God raised him from the dead, Jesus lives to help you, save you, redeem you, guide you, protect you, strengthen you, heal you, and prepare you for your high calling in life.

What good news do you need to hear today?

That God lives and cares about you?

That God forgives and cleanses you from all sin and unrighteousness?

That God empowers you to love God and love your neighbor?

That God can use your life, your gifts, your talents, and your failures to bring hope and healing to someone?

That God is at work in the world, in the most surprising places, with the most amazing people, to bring reconciliation and righteousness and joy?

That God gives you the power to *sing for joy and live with hope?*

All of this is the good news of God, the Gospel of God, and the Gospel of the Lord Jesus Christ.

III.

In this chapter, I have tried to weave this "whole cloth" of the Gospel with strands from Torah, Prophets, Psalms, Jesus, Paul, and the Apostles. Here is the way I say it, listening to Moses and David, Isaiah and the Psalmist, Jesus, and Paul and Luke and John, to the women and the men, the young and the old, and the saint and the sinner:

This is the Gospel of God, the Good News of Jesus: God raised Jesus from the dead, affirming his life and ministry of unbounded love, offering this same Spirit of unbounded love to everyone, and promising a future of beloved community to the whole human race. Believe this good news and live in it.

This is the Good News!! This is the Gospel of God.

This is good news to the addict, to the homeless, and to the refugee seeking a new life. This is good news to the cancer patient, the Ukrainian soldier, and the senator trying to serve a very diverse country, with faithfulness and courage.

This is the Gospel for you and me today. Hear it. Believe it. Live it. Rejoice in it.

About the Author

Dwight A. Moody is an author, minister, scholar, professor, administrator, social entrepreneur, and media host. He has pastored churches in Indiana, Pennsylvania, Kentucky, and North Carolina, served as dean of the chapel and professor of religion at a liberal arts college, launched and led (as first president) the Academy of Preachers, and created the media initiative, "TheMeetingHouse: Conversations on Religion and American Life." He is currently the pastor of Providence Baptist Church in Hendersonville, North Carolina.

Dr. Moody is a graduate of Georgetown College and Southern Baptist Theological Seminary. In addition, he has studied at Jerusalem University College in Israel and the graduate school of Notre Dame University. He holds the Doctor of Philosophy degree in systematic theology for a dissertation on the doctrine of biblical inspiration.

Dr. Moody has taught at Duquesne University and LaRoche College, both in Pittsburgh, Pennsylvania, Kentucky Wesleyan College in Owensboro. Kentucky, Georgetown College and Baptist Seminary of Kentucky in Georgetown, Kentucky, and Asbury University in Wilmore, Kentucky. He is the author of 6 books and the general editor of the nine-volume series "Sermons from the National Festival of Young Preachers."

Dr. Moody has been married more than 50 years to his wife Jan. They have three grown children, two grandchildren, and a home on St. Simons Island, Georgia.

Printed in the United States
by Baker & Taylor Publisher Services